Wome   *eich*

"It is worthy of note that each of the remarkable women in Joanne Gilbert's, *Women of Valor: Polish Resisters to the Third Reich,* made a point of showing that her survival often depended on the actions of Gentiles—actions that too often tragically resulted in the Gentiles' executions. It took courage to live through these events. It took courage, compassion, and skill to listen to these stories, and to capture them. The journey that you will share in this book is well worth the efforts of the writer, the survivor, and the reader . . ."

> **—Professor Michael Berenbaum, PhD., rabbi, author, film maker, professor: American Jewish University**

"I enjoyed reading the too-long-unsung stories of women who defied the Nazis in Joanne Gilbert's book, *Women of Valor: Polish Resisters to the Third Reich.* Manya Auster Feldman has been one of my heroes ever since I was honored to meet her many years ago. That Gilbert has so sensitively and effectively captured the voice and spirit of each of these extraordinary women is an achievement worthy of praise."

> **—Charles Silow, PhD., clinical psychologist, director of the Jewish Senior Life of Metropolitan Detroit's Program for Holocaust Survivors and Families**

"To call them 'Women of Valor' perfectly describes what they did: they stood up to the greatest evil we saw in the 20th century and maybe any century. Joanne Gilbert has told us a story that is little known and incredibly inspiring, and she has told it with love, verve, insight, and thorough research."

> **—Dr. Michael Green, PhD., author, history professor: University of Nevada/Las Vegas**

WOMEN OF VALOR

Polish Resisters to the Third Reich

Joanne D. Gilbert, M.Ed
CSN Faculty

Gihon River Press

Women of Valor: Polish Resisters to the Third Reich

GIHON RIVER PRESS
P.O. Box 88
East Stroudsburg PA 18301
www.gihonriverpress.com

Publisher's Cataloging-In-Publication Data
(Prepared by The Donohue Group, Inc.)

Gilbert, Joanne D.
Women of valor. Polish resisters to the Third Reich /
Joanne D. Gilbert, M.Ed.—First Gihon River Press edition.
    pages ; cm
Includes bibliographical references.
ISBN: 978-0-9819906-4-4 (paperback)
ISBN: 978-0-9890841-3-0 (eBook)
1. World War, 1939–1945—Underground movements—Poland—Biography.
2. World War, 1939-1945—Women—Poland—Biography. 3. World War, 1939–
1945—Participation, Female. 4. Anti-Nazi movement—Poland—Biography.
5. Women—Poland—History—20th century. 6. Poland—History—Occupation,
1939–1945. I. Title. II. Title: Polish resisters to the Third Reich

D802.P65 G55 2014   943.8/053/0922

First Edition
Gihon River Press
Printed in the United States of America

A Woman of Valor . . .
is robed in Strength and Dignity
and faces the Future with Grace

PROVERBS: 31

Contents

Foreword

There is a scene in the final film of the Permanent Exhibition of the United States Holocaust Memorial Museum in which a plump, elderly Jewish woman, speaking with a heavy Yiddish accent, counts "one . . . two . . . three," while slowly holding up her fingers, one at a time. It takes the viewer a couple of seconds to grasp the meaning of her words as she recounts her perilous escapades as a resistance fighter in the Sobibor Death Camp uprising in October—1943. It is hard for the viewer to reconcile the image of this gentle, kindly grandmother with the stark story of her actions during the deadly revolt against the Germans. It is difficult to envision her daring—and successful—escape from a death camp where some 250,000 Jews had been murdered. And as she lifts each finger, it is especially daunting to envision her decision to exact a price on her oppressors: taking the lives of three SS officials.

I kept thinking of this image as I read Joanne Gilbert's four stories of Jewish women who resisted the Germans. When you look at the images of them today as 80–90 year-old grandmothers: a retired Hebrew School teacher, a renowned photographer, a research-scientist, and a pious, thrice-widowed Brooklyn fine-artist, you could never imagine the dramatic stories behind their survival. Had these stories not been told with care and respect for accuracy, the reader might imagine that they were the stuff of fable, and not the lot of four young girls who had been thrown into a world of death and destruction. And while they had had no choice about their newly brutal circumstances, their choice to resist oppression, despite their lack of personal power, provides us with necessary, important, and inspiring lessons.

"Just because Jews were powerless
does not mean that they were passive."

This sage observation of David Marwell, a Holocaust historian and director of New York's Museum of Jewish Heritage, epitomizes the widely unknown actions of anti-Nazi resisters. For many years the image of the Jews was of pure passivity in the face of destruction. Others who were not there were often embarrassed by that perceived passivity, ashamed of the survivors, and perplexed that they did not fight back. Over time, we have come to understand the varieties of Jewish actions and also to appreciate the difficult—if not choiceless—choices that the victims faced. I teach my students at the American Jewish University that premature judgments are most often immature judgments with little appreciation for how dire the circumstances.

The women you will read about in Gilbert's book showed time and again, even before they became resistance fighters, that despite their lack of power, they refused to be passive. And they exhibited a variety of resistance actions. They were willing to give up all that they knew, including their own identities, to move from town to town, from situation to situation, and from the unknown to the unimaginable. That these young women defied the odds and survived is a tribute to their ability to maintain their humanity despite the overpowering forces that were determined to destroy them. These four young women were essentially powerless—but they refused to be passive. They could not have known at the time that their thoughts and actions occurred within specific, identifiable, stages of human resistance to oppression.

Swiss historian Werner Rings (1910-1998) identified four stages of resistance practiced in every country under German occupation: *Symbolic Resistance, Polemical Resistance, Self-Help* and in the end—but only in the end—*Armed Resistance. Symbolic Resistance* included those efforts to deny the enemy their goal. For Jews, it often consisted of spiritual defiance, secretly maintaining religious practices and cultural traditions. Another example was their determination to remain humane, giving to one another under conditions that pushed individuals toward their limits and threatened to turn one against the other in the lonely battle for survival. *Symbolic Resistance* could be even more basic, like the inmate who washed his clothes in filthy water and put them on wet to remind him that he once wore clean clothes each morning. And Primo Levi, perhaps the most keen observer of human nature in the camps, wrote of his friend Lorenzo, "But Lorenzo was a man. His humanity was pure and uncontaminated; he was outside this world of negation. Thanks to Lorenzo, I managed not to forget that I myself was a man."

Polemical Resistance involves using strong verbal or written arguments to show the fallacy of an opponent's position. This came easily to the Jews, who had practiced it for centuries. Newspapers and pamphlets were published, diaries were kept, and archives were created and hidden so that history would have a true record of what happened. Even humor became a form of *Polemical Resistance*, enabling victims to laugh at their oppressors and even at themselves and their conditions.

Self-Help Resistance was widely practiced in every theater of German occupation and under all conditions. Some Jews who were helped by non-Jews, went into hiding—sometimes for years. Others were able to pass as non-Jews. Even in the ghettos, Jews participated in *Self-Help* by setting up hidden schools and theater groups. In the Kovno ghetto there was a charity drive, gathering clothing and food for the poor. In Hungary, the Zionist underground copied the "safe-passes" that had been given out by Swiss diplomat Raul Wallenberg. These forgeries were then distributed throughout Budapest, where they made the difference between life and death. Even in the death camps, there were "camp sisters," the families that were formed providing support that often gave a prisoner the incentive to live, instead of turning into a *Musselman* (a starved and barely living skeleton), who was ready to die. Recently discovered evidence of the mass graves in the German-occupied territories of the Soviet Union also show that even in dying, there was resistance. It was apparent that some of the dead died without a wound to their bodies. How so? Fathers protected their sons, mothers their daughters, husbands their wives by pushing their loved ones into mass graves and taking the bullets intended for them. Of those buried alive beneath the heaps of corpses, a very few did manage to escape the death pits.

These earlier stages of resistance required as much courage and discipline as the latter—they not only denied the enemy the triumph of their efforts to dehumanize and to destroy the individual's soul, but also bolstered the communal spirit of an oppressed people. Dehumanization was essential to the destruction process. It is much easier to kill a woman or a man who has given up—who has despaired of life—than it is to destroy one who is valiantly defending his or her existence.

The fourth stage, *Armed Resistance*, was much more common than has been widely recognized. Jews fought on every front in the ghettos and in the forests. At first Jewish resistance fighters intuited—and later clearly understood—that the Germans wanted to annihilate the Jews. Thus, they had to resist either in armed uprisings or escape to the forests—or even by giving their children away to strangers before the ghettos were liquidated, and their captives transported to their deaths. Their armed resistance predated that of the non-Jewish population's Warsaw Uprising of 1944, which struck out against the Germans as the Red Army stood on the edge of the Vistula River. There were uprisings in three death camps: Treblinka and Sobibor, and even within crematoria of Birkenau, the death camp at Auschwitz.

Jews fought openly as integrated members of both the Yugoslavian and French resistance; clandestinely as part of antisemitic partisan units within the occupied Soviet Union; and in separate units in Poland as well as the forests in Soviet territories. While the first image of a resistance fighter typically is a man with a gun, women often fought alongside men, and were integral to resistance efforts in all theaters of operation. A crucial factor in their necessary and effective resistance activities was their linguistic skill. They acquired this advantage because, unlike the boys who commonly attended religious schools where Yiddish was the language of instruction, the girls often attended public schools.

In addition to learning their country's native language and customs, they also had the opportunity to meet and interact with Gentiles. Furthermore, their bodies did not immediately reveal the fact that they were Jews. Since Jewish boys were circumcised—the only circumcised men in many parts of Europe—they were particularly vulnerable to discovery. So females—especially if they had blue eyes and blonde hair—had some advantages over males when it came to passing as non-Jews. And since it was easier for Jewish women to blend in with non-Jews, they served as couriers and as scouts, and went out to get food and medicine for their families, as well as for hidden Jews and partisans.

Women, however, did face a different type of vulnerability. In the fighting camps, unprotected women could be subject to assault, because some male fighters thought that a woman's body was theirs as a reward. Often, their only safety depended on pairing up with a protective male. This was the case for Miriam Brysk, who along with her mother, was protected by her surgeon father's unique stature, and was therefore extraordinarily valuable to the partisans. Women also had to demonstrate their value to the combat unit either as fighters or as indispensable workers and nurses, who could pull their weight through perilous times. In the case of Faye Schulman, her value as a photographer and nurse, ensured her the respect and protection of the other partisans.

I found myself particularly drawn to the four women that Joanne Gilbert has portrayed. I was already familiar with Miriam's story because I wrote the Introduction to her book, *Amidst the Silence of Trees*. Hearing her voice again in a more condensed fashion only underscored the poignant story of her own interrupted childhood. She had learned to "obey orders," to keep quiet as instructed, to avoid all the things in life that ordinary six year old girls take for granted. Although she was protected by her father and her mother, she was forced to become a mini-adult, otherwise she could not survive. I was attracted to Lola's story because I had recently read her brother Ben Lesser's memoir, *Living a Life that Matters: From Nazi Nightmare to American Dream*. In describing his own tale of struggle and survival, Ben spoke often of his brave sister, and her equally courageous husband, who had saved the family time and again. Reading the story of their reunion from two entirely different perspectives only reinforces the strength and the importance of each story. Coincidentally, as I am now working in Lola's community in Boro Park, the home of many devout Hasidic communities in the United States, I have come to appreciate not only the courage of her actions during the Holocaust, but also the courage of her life of faith in its aftermath.

It is also worthy of note that these women each made a point of showing how their survival often depended on the actions of Gentiles—actions that too often resulted in executions. Read these stories and learn about these seemingly ordinary women, whose current appearance is deceptively simple— understand that the story and the lessons beneath each story are poignant and powerful. It took courage to live through these events and it takes courage, compassion, and skill to listen to these stories and to capture them. But the journey that you will share in this book is well worth the efforts of the writer and the survivor, and exceedingly valuable for you, their cherished readers.

DR. MICHAEL BERENBAUM
Los Angeles, California

To the Reader

On September 1, 1939, under the leadership of its Chancellor, Adolf Hitler, Nazi Germany invaded Poland, thereby triggering World War II. For the next six years, Germany's unparalleled reign of terror throughout Europe would focus on the extermination of Europe's Jews. This systematic, industrialized genocide that Hitler referred to as "The Final Solution to the Jewish Question," would become known thereafter as The Holocaust *or* The Shoah.

It is not widely known that Hitler also planned to enslave the Gentile people of Poland. Against the superior strength and unprecedented brutality of Germany's Third Reich, prospects for Polish Gentile and Jewish survival seemed all but impossible.

Despite the overwhelming odds, however, and despite the terror and the sacrifices, there were countless people—both Jewish and Gentile—who did dare to defy Hitler. And many of them were women.

Would you be surprised to learn that, unlike most people during World War II, there were many Jewish and non-Jewish (Gentile) women who risked monstrous torture and execution in order to oppose the Nazis? Would you be further surprised to learn that some of these amazing women not only survived, but went on to live long, productive lives, dedicated to human rights? While their selfless valor has remained largely unknown and uncelebrated throughout the seventy years following World War II, we are fortunate that some of them, now in their late 80s and 90s, are at last telling their extraordinary stories.

Women of Valor: Polish Resisters to the Third Reich is the first in a series of books celebrating the remarkable Jewish and Gentile women who put themselves in mortal danger by defying the Nazis between 1939 and 1945. Subsequent books will feature women who resisted the Nazis in France, the Netherlands, and Germany. The series includes rare, first-person interviews with valiant female resisters and partisans. Their extraordinary stories offer a unique perspective on the indomitable women who overcame brutal odds to fight for a common cause: the survival of humanity in the face of Hitler's virulently anti-Semitic (anti-Jewish) Third Reich. In telling their stories now, these women shed much-needed light on three simple questions that have been unnecessarily shrouded in complicated darkness for far too long:

1. Did the Polish Jews go to their deaths without putting up a fight?
2. Did any Polish Gentiles help the Jews?
3. Did Polish Jewish and Gentile women defy the Nazis?

The purpose of the *Women of Valor* series is not just to explore possible answers to these complex questions, but also to inspire further questions, as well as further answers. These true stories challenge us to re-examine our previous notions about Jews only as victims, and about Gentiles only as bystanders and perpetrators. By enabling us to consider past and present genocides within a reality-based perspective, they show us the importance of recognizing the earliest signs of oppression, and taking effective action against it before it's too late.

Over the past four years, I have been blessed to meet with—and to learn from—many of these remarkable women. I am profoundly grateful for their honesty, generosity, warmth, patience, and encouragement. In graciously reliving their often painful experiences so that others might learn the truth, they continue to fight genocide. While there is no way to adequately thank them for sharing their stories with me, I hope this book is worthy of their trust, and inspires others to carry on their legacy. Please join me in celebrating these "ordinary" women who did "extraordinary" things.

JOANNE D. GILBERT, M.ED
Las Vegas, Nevada
2014

WOMEN OF VALOR

Polish Resisters to the Third Reich

The world is a dangerous place
not because of those who do evil . . .
but because of those who look on
and do nothing.
ALBERT EINSTEIN (1879–1955)
German-Jewish-American Physicist

Introduction

Most of the world was stunned on September 1, 1939, when Hitler's Nazi Germany, employing its infamous *Blitzkrieg*, or "lightning war," attacked and invaded Poland, thereby launching World War II. This was particularly shocking because dynamic and democratic Germany was at that time respected as one of the most highly cultured nations in Western Europe. It was unimaginable that this sophisticated republic, which had been the birthplace of world-renowned scientists, artists, composers, writers, and philosophers,[1] and which, up until World War I, had enjoyed the best economy in Europe, could also be the birthplace and control center of Adolph Hitler's monstrous Third Reich. Tragically, this international inability to even *imagine* the horrors of the approaching Nazi Holocaust was one of the very reasons that it was able to happen. How could anyone prepare for the unimaginable? Some could not believe it even while it was happening. More tragic is the fact that this horror could have been prevented, or at least substantially diminished, if other governments, such as Great Britain and the

---

1. Some illustrious pre-World War II Germans included *musicians*: George Handel (1685–1759), Johann Sebastian Bach (1685–1750), Ludwig van Beethoven (1770–1827), German-Jewish Felix Mendelssohn (1809–1847), Robert Schumann (1810–1856), Richard Strauss (1864–1949), Johannes Brahms (1883–1897); *writers*: Johann von Goethe (1749–1832), Jacob Grimm (1785–1863), Wilhelm Grimm (1786–1859), Heinrich Heine (1797–1856), Hermann Hesse (1877–1962); *inventors*: Johannes Gutenberg (1398–1468), Immanuel Kant (1724–1804), Gottlieb Wilhelm Daimler (1834–1900); *philosophers*: German-Jewish Moses Mendelssohn (1729–1786), Arthur Schopenhauer (1788-1860), Thomas Mann (1875–1955); *artists*: Albrecht Dürer (1471–1528), Oskar Schlemmer (1888–1943), Max Ernst (1891–1976); *scientists*: Johannes Kepler (1571–1630), Daniel Gabriel Fahrenheit (1686–1736), German-Jewish Albert Einstein (1879–1955); *psychologist*: Carl Jung (1875–1961).

United States—which had known early on what the Germans were doing—
had chosen to fight them sooner.[2]

As horrifying as Germany's invasion of Poland was to others, it was totally
logical and glorious to Hitler and his followers. One reason for this was Germany's historically accepted philosophy of *Lebensraum* ("life room" or "living
space"). This notion, which had actually existed long before Hitler came to
power, asserted that Germany had the indisputable right to expand its territory, whenever and however necessary, in order to support the needs of its
growing population. It promoted the right of the "superior" Aryan[3] German
people to displace, and even eliminate, "inferior" races. This acceptability of
purging undesirables in order to protect superior German blood from con-
tamination by inferior races, would soon help justify Hitler's campaign to
eliminate the Jews of Europe.

Hitler's sense of entitlement was further reinforced by what Germans considered to be the excessively punitive terms of the 1919 Versailles Treaty,[4]
which had been signed after the Armistice ending World War I. Hitler believed that the Jews were responsible for the "unfair" anti-German elements
of this treaty. Many defeated Germans were outraged at being required to pay
massive reparations to the victorious Allies, particularly to France and Belgium, which had suffered devastating losses. Germans were also infuriated
that the requirement to disarm their military left them vulnerable to attackers. And they were especially upset at being forced to forfeit what they considered "German" land to Poland. Germany felt that it had every right to
reclaim this territory, referring to it as the "reunification" of Germany. Hitler's

---

2. For details on the U.S. and British response to early reports of German atrocities, go to
http://www.ushmm.org/wlc/en/article.php?ModuleId=10005182

3. Hitler incorrectly used the word *Aryan* to describe his Nordic, blond, blue-eyed ideal of
a German Master Race. He believed that the Germans were *ubermenschen* or superior people.
The people who Hitler designated as "inferior" were known in German as *untermenschen,*
meaning "lower-people" or "sub-humans." Jews were considered "non-human."

4. The Versailles Treaty, signed between the defeated Germany and the victorious Allies in
1919, required Germany to accept responsibility and punishment for the war. Since the Germans were not invited to the meeting where the Allies developed the treaty's terms, the actual
treaty was dictated to them. This inevitably created the German nationalistic rage that Hitler
exploited in order to start World War II. This rage was not shared by the other Central Power
countries because they signed separate, less punitive treaties.

racial-purity policies, along with *Lebensraum,* and Germany's disregard of the Versailles Treaty, were further galvanized by technological advances of the time.[5] The result of this lethal combination was the first government-sanctioned, industrialized genocide in history. It is a tribute to the strength of the human mind, body, and spirit that so many Polish Jews and Gentiles, facing impossible odds and possessing few resources, refused to passively accept what seemed to be the inevitable victory of the Third Reich.

Now, over seventy years later, as these last Nazi resisters are losing their battle with time, it is important to learn as much as we can from them directly. By trying to put ourselves in their place and learn from their experiences, we can assess our own capacity to recognize and defeat oppression. Imagine, if you can, that your own community has suddenly been invaded by an all-powerful and evil enemy. Their goal is to enslave or destroy you, and everyone you know and love.

- Would you accept your fate?
- Would you risk your life to defy a murderous enemy?
- Would you collaborate with the enemy in order to save yourself?
- Would you risk death to protect your loved ones?
- Would you help terrified strangers?

These were some of the challenges that confronted hundreds of thousands of Polish women—both Jewish and Gentile—between 1939 and 1945, when their country was invaded and occupied by Nazi Germany. And while they faced starvation, diseases, torture, and death, just as did the men, their challenges and choices were often very different. Men had traditionally been expected to fight when necessary to protect their families, homes, and countries,

---

5. Particularly effective was Hitler's use of the mass media, including radio, loudspeakers, and motion pictures to spread the propaganda that controlled and manipulated the masses. At his huge rallies, special sound and lighting effects were used to flood the audiences' senses. Other technological advantages that benefitted Hitler were related to transportation. He made very effective use of his airplane, to commute quickly to various meetings and events, thereby enabling him to speak to more audiences. Particularly horrific was Hitler's use of Europe's efficient train system in deporting millions of innocent people to extermination camps. Many historians agree that the Holocaust could not have happened without the benefit of these trains.

so their role in resistance was socially acceptable. Women, on the other hand, had traditionally been trained to be housewives, and to expect their men to fight when necessary, to protect them. Traditional society did not provide similar support for female fighters. Unlike women in free countries today, whose thoughts might be filled with family, education, career, hobbies, and plans for the future, women in German-occupied Poland were focused on enduring a sudden, deadly, enemy invasion and occupation. Their thoughts were about surviving, and protecting their families against a seemingly end-less and unfathomable horror. They had no special self-defense skills or knowledge of fighting against military invaders. Before the German invasion, they'd been living "normal" lives with "normal" activities, duties, challenges, hopes, and dreams. On September 1, 1939, however, every semblance of normal life for Polish Jewish and Gentile women ceased to exist.

It is not widely known Hitler's first targets were the Polish people. In a speech the week before Germany invaded Poland, Hitler commanded his forces to show the utmost cruelty toward the Poles, "to kill without pity or mercy all men, women, and children of the Polish race or language," so that the land would be clean enough for Germans to inhabit.[6] Able-bodied Polish Gentile men were quickly conscripted into the German military, often to fight against their own countrymen. Many others were sent to forced-labor or concentration camps. Now controlled by enemy invaders, Polish cities and towns became deathtraps. Food, medicine, and basic commodities were ra-tioned so severely that starvation, disease, and crime were rampant. With most of the men gone, women took on life-threatening responsibilities, not only for saving themselves, but also their loved ones and neighbors. In many cases, they even helped strangers who were in desperate need. Since the peo-ple of an enemy-occupied country are victims of tyranny, it was all but im-possible for anyone to rebel in any way. It was nothing short of a miracle that despite the odds, so many did rebel.

As bad as life became for the Poles, life for Polish Jews became even worse. Jewish businesses, bank accounts, homes, and belongings were confiscated. Jews were often terrorized, beaten, forced into slave labor, taken to concen-

---

6. Lukas, Richard C. (2013). *Out of the Inferno: Poles Remember the Holocaust.* University Press of Kentucky. p. 2.

tration and extermination camps, or just murdered on the spot. Those who remained alive were crowded into squalid, prison-like *ghettos*,[7] where deadly *aktions* were routine. Some Jews, however, wearing only the clothes on their backs, fled to the forests, where they learned how to survive on their own, or in family camps. Still others became partisans, and learned how to fight— and how to kill.

Even the most minor anti-Nazi resistance in Poland was considered to be terrorism by the Germans, and was dealt with accordingly: execution. Despite the danger, however, acts of resistance were innumerable and varied, ranging from the "spiritual," such as:

- practicing one's religion in small, secret ways
- providing moral support to victims, resisters, and rescuers
- sharing food/clothes with others in need
- neglecting, avoiding, or forgetting to denounce or turn in a Jew

to the "passive," or non-violent, such as:

- making illegal detailed journals for later documentation
- hiding valuables instead of turning them in
- refusing to buy German products
- refusing to cooperate with minor laws
- reading/hiding/sharing forbidden publications
- keeping/hiding/listening to a forbidden radio
- creating and maintaining small, hidden schools and libraries

and on to "active," and when necessary, violent resistance, such as:

- organizing/hosting/attending resistance meetings
- raising money for resistance activities

---

7. As far back as the early 1500s in Venice, Italy, the area of the city where Jews were forced to live was called a *ghetto*. Other major European cities created Jewish ghettos in the 1600s and 1700s. During the Third Reich, Jews were forced out of their homes into ghettos which were overcrowded, squalid, disease-ridden, virtual prisons, where they were brutalized and starved before being killed or deported to extermination camps.

- making/distributing anti-German flyers
- forging ID and ration cards
- hiding/operating a radio to communicate with the Allies
- decoding/delivering messages
- being a messenger (courier) of important information, documents, medications, food
- passing as a German in order to spy on them
- hiding/feeding/transporting Jews
- acting on behalf of Jews as the owner of their businesses
- becoming foster parents to Jewish children
- escaping to the forests
- becoming a partisan
- sabotaging German weapons factories, food-production/storage facilities, communication networks, military operations
- blowing up German roads, buildings, and bridges
- engaging in physical combat
- killing Germans and their collaborators

And of course, the greatest resistance action of all: *surviving the German horror.*

Since the German objectives were to exterminate the Jews and to enslave the Poles, almost any normal human activity could have been, and all too often was, considered grounds for execution. In fact, the actual condition of being alive could be considered by some to be an act of defiance. Since so few Polish Gentiles and Jewish active resisters survived, their heroic acts, from the very personal determination to live another day, to the selfless combat of the partisans, usually went unrecognized and uncelebrated.

It is only in recent years that the extraordinary exploits, sacrifices and achievements of heroic male anti-German resisters such as the Bielski brothers, Abba Kovner, Oscar Schindler, Jan Karski, and Raoul Wallenberg,[8] have

---

8. In 1942, Jewish brothers *Tuvia* (1906–1987), *Alexander* (1912–1995), *Asael* (1908–1945), and *Aron* (1927–) *Bielski* organized their own partisan group in the Naliboki Forest in what is now Belarus. *Abba Kovner* (1918–1987) was a young Jewish partisan leader in Vilna, Lithuania. *Oscar Schindler* (1908–1974), a German Gentile businessman, saved the lives of 1200 Jews by employing them in his factories in what was then Poland. *Jan Karski* (1914–2000) was a highly educated Polish-Catholic diplomat turned resistance leader and fighter who reported the facts of German atrocities to the Allies as early as 1942. Tragically, his reports

been chronicled and celebrated in books and movies. Unlike men, however, women during the 1930s and 40s were not typically business owners, diplomats, or physically powerful rebels. Women's conventional, socially-approved roles, which largely focused on their families and homes, were all but invisible. This by no means meant that they were not active participants in anti-Nazi resistance. On the contrary, their very *invisibility* would ironically prove to be an asset, because in order to avoid being discovered, female resistance activities had to be as invisible as possible.

How did post-World War I Poland, a country rich in natural resources and growing in sophistication, a country in which Jews had historically been more welcome than in any other in Europe, also become the country where its Gentile population would be enslaved and its Jewish population eliminated? What was it about Poland and the Jewish people that made this often-embattled land so central to Hitler's Final Solution?

---

were ignored. *Raoul Wallenberg* (1912–1947?) was a Swedish-Gentile architect, businessman, and diplomat who rescued tens of thousands Jews from German-occupied Hungary.

"Poland is still coming to terms with what happened to its Jewish community during World War II."

ADAM EASTON, BBC News Correspondent, on the Commemoration of the
70th Anniversary of the Warsaw Ghetto Uprising,
April 19, 2013, Warsaw, Poland

Chapter 1

A Brief History of Poland and the Jewish People

The history of the Jewish people in Poland is long and complex, stretching back almost 1,000 years. Throughout this time, attitudes toward Jews were divided along class lines. The predominantly Catholic peasant population, which was profoundly influenced by the anti-Jewish teachings of the Church, did not usually welcome Jews. The wealthy and powerful nobles, however, seeing the need for Jewish merchants, doctors, and skilled tradesmen to function as a middle class, often welcomed Jews to their estates and nearby villages. The earliest Jews in Poland were probably traders who traveled throughout Europe and Asia. Centrally located, Poland was a convenient place for these traders to stop and establish their own homes. While the "Kingdom of Poland," under King Bolesław I the Brave, was officially founded in 1025 CE, Poland did have status as a state as far back as 966 CE, under its ruler, Mieszko I. And apparently, at least one Jewish person spent some time there: Abraham ben Jacob, who wrote about Poland and Mieszko in his journal.[9] Throughout the ensuing centuries, Poland was periodically conquered, victimized, and exploited by its most recent invader. Often partitioned and parceled off, Poland sometimes wasn't even a country, as it was bounced back and forth between competing governments. During this time, there was always a Jewish population whose living conditions fluctuated depending upon the whims of the various rulers.

In 1098, a huge wave of European Jews, who were fleeing the widespread brutality of the First Crusade, found refuge in Poland. At that time, the Jews were welcomed in Poland because their many commercial, managerial, mercantile, legal, medical, and financial skills provided a much-needed link between the nobility and the peasants. This positive relationship between Polish Gentiles and Jews was tested in the mid-1300s, however, when another massive wave of European Jews came to Poland because they were being blamed for the murderous Black Death, also known as the Bubonic Plague. Estimates of the plague's death toll vary widely, but generally fall between 75 million and 200 million people.

Ignorant of basic sanitary practices and the biological reasons for the plague, terrified Europeans looked for a scapegoat. When it appeared as if fewer Jews were dying of the disease, many Gentiles decided that the plague was part of a Jewish plot to eliminate Christians. The widespread belief that the only way to remove the plague was to remove the Jews, resulted in the massacres of thousands of Jews throughout Europe. Ironically, it was the more sanitary lifestyle mandated by Jewish law that helped Jews avoid the filth, fleas, and rats that carried the disease. And paradoxically, Poland, with its large population of Jews, was largely spared from the plague. Despite Poland's seeming immunity to the disease, however, Jews there were still considered responsible, and many became victims of deadly anti-Jewish *pogroms* or riots.

By the 1500s, however, Polish Jews were once again welcome in Poland, and remained actively involved in all areas of society until the late 1700s. Depending upon the policies of its varying rulers, and the conditions of the Jews throughout Russia and Europe, Poland was relatively tolerant of its Jews until the 1770s. At this time, Poland once again was partitioned by a series of anti-Semitic occupying governments. And in the 1790s, Russia's Catherine

---

9. *Abraham ben Jacob* was an Arabic/Sephardi/Jewish merchant who traveled as far as Rome and met the Pope. (See: www.encyclopedia.com/doc/1G2-2830902123.html)

the Great decided to create the "Pale of Settlement,"[10] the massive, forced relocation of Russia's Jews to its western territories. Much of this region had formerly been part of Poland. The great influx of Jews into these already economically depressed areas was a source of hostility against the newcomers, most of whom were impoverished.

In the midst of this very precarious situation, these newly-arrived Jews created their own villages, known as *shtetles*, wherein they conducted traditional Jewish lives, spoke *Yiddish*, and kept to themselves. Since Poland was predominantly Catholic, and still profoundly influenced by the Church's historic anti-Semitic teachings, Jews hoped that, "if we don't bother them, maybe they won't bother us." Tragically, their hopes were too often futile, and the shtetles were regularly subjected to savage, merciless *pogroms*.

The end of World War I also marked the end of the Pale, and most of its land, including its large population of Jews, became part of the newly independent country of Poland: a country quickly patched together by the Allies from parts of the now dissolved German, Austro-Hungarian, and Russian Empires. Fearing their powerful and aggressive Soviet Communist neighbors, however, and believing—incorrectly—that there was an anti-Christian partnership between Communists and Jews, ruthless anti-Semitism in Poland soon became more and more pervasive. The protections of Jews and other minorities that had been mandated by the Versailles Treaty were not enforced, and deadly *pogroms* proliferated.

Despite the many obstacles, however, Jewish communities throughout Poland were committed to maintaining a sense of normalcy, as well as Jewish cultural and religious continuity. There were over 30 daily newspapers, and more than 130 Jewish periodicals printed in Yiddish, Hebrew, and Polish.[11] Many urban Jews also spoke German, Russian, Hungarian, and even French. Jews were well-represented in the professions and the arts, and there were many Jewish schools, synagogues, clubs, and theaters. Jewish political parties, such as the *Bund*, and various *Zionist* groups were active, and some Communist and

---

10. *The Pale of Settlement* was the far western territory of Russia, including former territories of Lithuania, Belarus, and Poland, where Russia's Jews were forced to live. The word "Pale" comes from the Latin for *palus* meaning an enclosed area.

11. For more information go to: The Jewish Virtual Library at www.jewishvirtuallibrary.org/jsource/vjw/Poland.html

Socialist political groups included both Gentiles and Jews. This era of mutual tolerance, like those before, however, would soon be challenged by another wave of virulent anti-Semitism.

Following the 1929 Stock Market Crash in the United States, a worldwide economic Great Depression grew, and Poland, which was still reeling from the human and financial costs of World War I, was particularly hard-hit. As had all too often been the case in times of massive economic hardships, whose real origins people did not understand, many Poles felt the Jews were responsible. And after 1933, anti-Semitism in Poland was further aroused by the anti-Semitism so prevalent in Germany. In fact, after 1935, Poland began to implement laws similar to Germany's severely restrictive, anti-Semitic Nuremberg Laws.[12] Jewish shops had to include the owner's name on the store's sign, making them easier to boycott and vandalize. The number of Jews allowed in the civil service, universities, and the professions, including medicine and law, was severely limited, and ultimately, Jews were totally barred from those occupations. Looking for ways to rid Poland of its Jews, the Polish government even investigated the possibility of shipping them to the island of Madagascar, which is located in the Indian Ocean, to the southeast of Africa, an idea that would later also be considered by the Germans.[13] Unable to work, or protect their own businesses and possessions, the economic status of Poland's Jews plunged, and their lives became increasingly desperate.

Poland's interwar independence would be short-lived. In fact, the Germans and the Soviets were making plans for Poland long before World War II broke out. In August 1939, under the terms of the German-Soviet Non-Aggression Pact,[14] at some unspecified time in the near future, Poland was to be occupied

---

12. In 1935, at the annual Nazi meeting, the brutal anti-Jewish *Nuremberg Laws* were officially adopted by the German government. In defining who was a Jew, these laws took German citizenship and human rights away from Jews.

13. The Poles had not invented this idea. It had already been considered by the Dutch and the British. For more information go to: Shoah Resource Center, The International School for Holocaust Studies Report at www.yadvashem.org

14. The *German-Soviet Non-Aggression Pact*, also known as the Molotov–Ribbentrop Pact, was named after the Soviet foreign minister Vyacheslav Molotov and the Nazi German foreign minister, Joachim von Ribbentrop. This pact guaranteed that the USSR and Germany would not attack each other, and temporarily awarded the eastern section of Poland to the Soviets. The Pact was important because it protected Germany from fighting on two fronts until it was

Europe 1933

Poland 1933

by Nazi Germany in the West and the Soviets in the East. In preparation for their September 1939 invasion, the Germans had compiled a list of more than 60,000 Polish leaders, including aristocrats, politicians, scholars, scientists, doctors, lawyers, writers, musicians, artists, government officials, prisoners of war, and other "undesirables," who were targeted for early elimination. The Nazis planned to round up and remove these leaders, so that the rest of the population would be demoralized and easier to control, both mentally and physically. So on September 1, 1939, when the Germans occupied western and central Poland, they knew exactly which Poles to eliminate first. The way was paved for the earliest German mass murders by mobilized killing squads, known as *Einsatzkommandos* that were sent in advance of the infantry. The next German target would be young, able-bodied Polish men who were either conscripted into the German military, or sent to forced-labor camps.

Since the first people to be conspicuously victimized by the Germans were Polish Gentiles, it looked to them as if the Jews—who at that time were "merely" being forced out of their homes to go live in ghettos—were receiving preferential treatment. The belief that the Jews had struck some kind of bargain with the Germans intensified Poland's anti-Semitism. So despite, or perhaps even because of, the victimization of Polish Gentiles at the hands of the Germans, Polish anti-Semitism escalated. It became even more pervasive during the time of the German-Soviet Non-Aggression Pact (1939–1941), because many Jews believed that any government would be better than the Germans, and fled to the Soviet sector. Poles, who already deeply resented the Soviets for historic border conflicts and aggressive communist government, interpreted this Jewish flight as an alignment with the Communists against the Poles, and felt betrayed. Further anti-Semitism continued to be endorsed by many of the Catholic Churches, where Jews were still categorized as "Christ-Killers."

So with the German invasion of western Poland on September 1, 1939, and the Soviet invasion of eastern Poland on September 17, 1939, Poland no longer existed as a country. It was split into two parts, and under the often conflicting jurisdictions of two governments that not only did not trust each other, but would soon be at war with each other. There was, however, a Polish government-in-exile in London, directing over three hundred clandestine

---

ready to continue its expansion to the east. Germany broke the pact with its attack (known as *Barbarossa*) on the USSR in June 1941.

agencies and military groups, including the Polish Home Army, which was formed in 1942. Also established were underground courts with the authority to arrest, try, and convict Nazi collaborators. And there was even a covert network of schools—from kindergarten through universities—that continued to operate during the German occupation. The major goal of the Polish government-in-exile was to keep its institutions functioning so that it would be able to resume normal operations as soon as the Germans were beaten by the Allies. Unfortunately, the aid from Poland's allies was too little and too late. And tragically, what at first seemed to be the latest in a long line of cruel foreign occupations, would instead result in Poland becoming the site of history's most heinous episode: the Holocaust.

In German-occupied Poland, Jews were required to wear Stars of David either on armbands or on badges sewn to both the front and the back of their clothing. Now that Jews were visible, they became easy targets for abuse, violence, and execution. All too soon, they would be rounded up and sent to die in the gas chambers such as those at Chelmno, Belzec, Sobibor, Treblinka, Majdanek, and Auschwitz-Birkenau. Since these activities kept the Nazis very busy, and required more and more territory, they soon became dissatisfied controlling only half of Poland. In June 1941, the Germans broke their Non-Aggression Pact with the Soviets, and took over all of Poland. Most of its central and southern regions became part of a large administrative area called the *German General Gouvernment*. Germany quickly turned this area into a vast prison system, encompassing a network of over four hundred concentration camps, along with numerous sub-camps. Filled with "undesirables," the purpose of these camps was to work and starve inmates to death, and executions were not uncommon. The Germans' campaign to relocate all of Europe's Jews to the newly formed prison-like ghettos in Poland first required that existing Polish Gentile residents be removed, causing them great hardship. Crowded together, and isolated from the outside world, the Jews would be easy to control, transport . . . and destroy.

In addition to the camps, there were at least one thousand Jewish ghettos in German-occupied Poland and the Soviet Union, the largest of which were in Warsaw, Lodz, Krakow, Bialystok, Lvov, and Lublin. These ghettos were typically located near railroad tracks and used as staging areas for Jewish deportation to extermination camps. Living conditions in the ghettos were appalling—not meant to be survived—with several families crowded into one-room apartments. Food rations were severely restricted and disease, especially typhus, was rampant. Black markets sprang up where food and medicines were secretly brought to the ghetto walls by Poles in exchange for whatever jewelry or other goods the Jews had managed to smuggle in. Some Jews, especially those who were blond and blue-eyed, were able to sneak out of the ghettos through the sewer systems, or a disguised hole in the fence, obtain needed food and supplies, and then sneak back into the ghetto. Many Jews were worked to death, while others starved and froze to death right on the streets. Sometimes after a particularly brutal *aktion*, the numerous corpses would be loaded in wheelbarrows and taken to the central square where they would be piled up into a high hill, then doused with gasoline and set on fire. Of the few Jews who were able to escape from ghettos, many were assisted by Poles who provided them with hiding places, forged documents, and food.

Polish Jews did not submit to their fate without constant resistance of various types. In addition to spontaneous, daily resistance, there were countless informal family and neighborhood groups, plus many previously established Jewish Communist and Zionist youth organizations. There were even some formally organized Jewish paramilitary resistance groups, such as the Jewish Fighting Organization, or ZOB (known in Polish as *Zydowska Organizacja*), and the Jewish Military League.

The earliest organized Polish resistance effort, the "Home Army," was under the jurisdiction of the Polish Underground State,[15] which had been established by the Polish government-in-exile, and included men, women, teenagers, and even children. Despite the risks, members of the resistance, whether working individually or with others, did whatever was necessary to achieve their goals.[16] In fact, one of its founders, Witold Pilecki (1901–1948), volunteered in 1941 for imprisonment in Auschwitz. Once inside, he organized a resistance movement in the camp and set up a communication network to let the Allies know what was going on. Unfortunately, his reports

---

15. *The Polish Underground State* was comprised of two components. One was the government-in-exile, located first in Paris and then in London. The other component was the Underground Army which fought clandestinely in what had once been Poland. While they worked closely together, many decisions had to be made independently by the group in Poland.

16. See "The Polish Underground State and The Home Army (1939–45)," by Dr. Marek Ney-Krwawicz (London Branch of the Polish Home Army Ex-Servicemen Association: www.polishresistance-ak.org)

were at first ignored. In addition to its military, and in contrast to every other European country, the Polish government-in-exile also established and supported a comprehensive relief organization specifically to help the Jews in September 1942. The Council to Aid Jews was known by its code name, *Zegota*, and was run by a partnership of Catholics and Jews, under the leadership of two dedicated Catholic resistance workers, Zofia Kossak-Szczucka and Wanda Krahelska-Filipowicz.

Before the 1939 German invasion, Poland's population of approximately thirty-five million included almost 3.5 million Jews, more than any other European country. In fact, for many centuries Poland had been considered the heart and center of Europe's Jewish population. When German occupation of Poland ended in 1945, over six million Poles—approximately half of which were Jews—had been annihilated. It is clear, however, that amidst the unspeakable horror and tragedy of the German Occupation, there was also immeasurable valor and victory, by both Polish Jews and Polish Gentiles. Widely unacknowledged, is that during World War II, despite Poland's (and Europe's) historic anti-Semitism, most Poles did not actively collaborate with the Nazis.[17] Also not widely known is that hundreds of Polish Gentiles were executed specifically because they helped Jews. And while the exact number will never be known, over six thousand "Righteous Gentiles" have so far been recognized by Israel's *Yad Vashem*.[18] Whether Polish Gentiles helped Jews as individuals, or as part of organizations, the risks they took ensured that some Jewish lives would be saved, and that new generations of Jews would be born.

Today, many people would be surprised to learn that the help went both ways. Some Jews supported Gentiles in opposing the Nazis by fighting in the Polish military and in the 1944 Warsaw Uprising. So there were thousands of people—Jewish and Gentile—who defied all the odds, risking their lives and everything and everyone they had ever loved, in order to defy the Nazis. Among them were many indomitable women, who did whatever was necessary in

---

17. Statistics from the Israeli War Crimes Commission indicate that less than 0.1% of Polish Gentiles collaborated with the Germans. (See Richard C. Lukas, *Out of the Inferno: Poles Remember the Holocaust*, University Press of Kentucky 1989, p. 13.)

18. In 1953, Israel established *Yad Vashem* (the *Holocaust Martyrs' and Heroes' Remembrance Authority*) in order to honor *Righteous Gentiles* who risked, and even sacrificed, their lives in order to help Jews. As of 2013, there were 6,394 Polish Righteous Gentiles.

order to further the cause of survival and freedom. Who were these women, who unlike so many others, recognized early on what the Germans were doing in Poland? Who were these women who fought for the truth, sometimes against their own families? Who were these women, who went against everything that they had been taught about women's place in society, in order to defy the Germans?

They were everyday women. They were grandmothers, wives, mothers, daughters, and sisters. Some were wealthy, some middle class, and some were impoverished. They lived in cities, villages, farms, and shtetles. They were housewives . . . they were professionals . . . they were farmers, nurses, clerks, storekeepers, bakers, domestic servants, and aristocrats. Together they lived in a country whose entire history was fraught with ethnic, social, economic, and geographic conflict. And by defying, surmounting, and surviving history's most heinous attack on humanity, they have added an extraordinary chapter to the legacy of women's historic resistance to oppression.

"Let us not go like sheep to the slaughter. . . . The only reply to a murderer is resistance. . . . it is better to die as free fighters than to live at the mercy of killers. Resist, resist, to our last breath."

ABBA KOVNER (1918–1987) Jewish Partisan leader, poet,
The First Call: Manifesto of Jewish Resistance
Vilna, Lithuania, December 31, 1941

Chapter 2

A Brief Overview of Polish Jewish and Gentile Female Resistance to Oppression

Despite being labeled historically—and inaccurately—as "the weaker sex," women have a long history of resisting oppression and fighting successfully for survival, even against seemingly impossible odds. Countless role models of courageous, strong, and successful women stand in striking contrast to their image of being inferior to men. There has never been a time when women did not take responsibility for resisting and overcoming challenges to their own safety and that of their loved ones and countries.

In terms of valiant Jewish women, there is of course, the famous tribute to "A Woman of Valor" in the Hebrew Bible, in which strong women are extolled as having value "far beyond pearls." One such Jewish woman was Deborah (the "Mother of Israel"), who as a prophetess and the only known female Israelite Judge, inspired a successful attack against the ancient Canaanites. Another Old Testament woman of valor was Queen Esther, who saved the

Jews from the evil Persian Haman. In sixteenth-century Spain, Jewish Donna Gracia Mendes (c.1510–1569) was known as "the Queen Esther of her time." As the head of a large banking empire, and a powerful activist for Jewish rights, Mendes helped save many Jewish victims of the Spanish Inquisition.

Hannah Verbermacher (1805–1888), also known as *The Maiden of Ludmir*, (c.1806–1888) was said to have defied strict *Hasidic* Jewish rules to become the only female Hasidic Rabbi in history. Sarah Aaronsohn (1890–1917) was born in a village in the Ottoman Empire (now in Israel's Haifa district), and after witnessing the horror of the Armenian massacres by the Turks, she became a spy for the British. She also worked tirelessly to create a Jewish homeland in Israel. Just a few of the incalculable number of Polish-Jewish heroines of World War II were Haika Grossman (1919–1996), a leader of the Jewish Underground, Eta Wrobel (1918–2008), who organized a partisan fighting unit in the forest, and Tosia Altman (1918–1943), who was a leader of the dauntless *kashariyot*,[19] underground couriers who traveled throughout German-occupied Europe. One of the many Jewish women who fiercely fought the Germans during the final uprising of the Warsaw Ghetto,[20] which took place from April 19–May 16, 1943, was Zivia Lubetkin (1914–1976), a top-ranked ZOB commander. The following year, she joined the city of Warsaw's uprising against the Germans, August 1–October 2, 1944.[21] After the war, she moved to Israel, where in 1949, she helped to establish the Ghetto Fighters' House Museum.

In Poland, Gentile women of valor have always been held in high esteem. The historic archetype of the *Matka Polka*, the revered "Mothers of Poland," represents the strength of women, not only in caring for and protecting their families, but also in taking up arms and fighting for the Polish people. Some of the many heroic Polish women role models include the fabled Princess

---

19. See: "Kashariyot (Couriers) in the Jewish Resistance during the Holocaust," by Lenore J. Weitzman, http://jwa.org/encyclopedia/article/kashariyot-couriers-in-jewish-resistance-during-holocaust

20. The final uprising of the Warsaw Ghetto was conducted under the direction of the Jewish Fighting Organization (ZOB) and the Jewish Fighting Union (ZZW), who decided to die fighting rather than passively accept their fate as the Germans liquidated the Warsaw Ghetto.

21. Warsaw was the only city in Europe that planned and implemented an armed uprising against the Germans. Conducted by the Polish Underground Army, this struggle attempted to liberate Warsaw and its 1,000,000 inhabitants. Many felt that their ultimate loss could have been prevented if the Allies had provided support.

Wanda (c. 8th century), who upon the death of her father, King Krakus, became Queen of the Poles. In the fourteenth century, Queen Jadwiga (c. 1373–1399) ruled Poland from 1384 to her death. Emilia Plater (1806–1831) was a Polish-Lithuanian aristocrat and revolutionary who fought for Poland in an 1830 uprising. Warsaw-born Maria Skłodowska (1867–1934), who became renowned as Madame Curie, eventually moved to France and was the first woman to win a Nobel Prize. In fact, she won two!

During the German-occupation, Wanda Krahelska-Filipowicz (1886–1968), who was the wife of a former ambassador to Washington D.C., not only sheltered Jews herself, but also used her social, military, and political connections to provide significant aid to Poland's Jews. A lifelong political activist, she was a respected leader of the anti-Nazi Polish Underground, and understood the necessity of centralizing all efforts to help Jews. Along with Zofia Kossak-Szczucka (1889–1968), a famous writer who was dedicated to fighting the Germans, Filipowicz helped to found Zegota. Szczucka was eventually arrested for aiding Jews, and sent to Auschwitz. Upon her release in 1944, she participated in the Warsaw Uprising. Also involved with Zegota, were Irena Sendlerova (1910–2008) and Matylda Getter (1870–1968). In 2009, Zofia Kossak-Szczucka, Irena Sendlerova, and Matylda Getter were honored by the Polish Mint with a special commemorative coin. As a member of the Polish Underground, Barbara Szymańska Makuch (1917–2004), also took great risks to aid Jews before being captured, and ultimately surviving incarceration in a concentration camp. Not widely known is the fact that almost five thousand Polish women, including some Jewish women, fought the Germans in the 1944 Warsaw Uprising.

In addition to the Jewish and Gentile women who defied the Germans in Poland, some Polish women went to England in order to join the British Special Operations Executive (SOE), a secret war department formed in 1940. The purpose of the SOE was to support underground resistance movements in German-occupied countries. These women were trained in combat, communications, parachuting, and assuming the identities of locals so they could blend in when sent to countries such as France, Poland, or Hungary. One of these daring women was Maria Krystyna Janina Skarbek (1908–1952), also known as Christine Granville. Born to a mixed Catholic-Jewish family, she was renowned for her bold secret missions into German-occupied Poland and France.

Ironically, the historically accepted assumptions of female weakness, i.e., that women, unlike men, could never be fighters—much less stealthy spies, dauntless couriers, and indomitable warriors—provided women with unique opportunities to resist the Germans that were not available to men. The Polish Jewish and Gentile women who defied the Nazis showed that their "weaknesses" were really strengths. They were courageous, resourceful, resilient, creative, intelligent, quick-witted, selfless, and independent. They were able to improvise on a moment's notice, using whatever was at hand to confront life or death challenges. It was their traditional role as secondary citizens that would make it almost impossible for women to be seen as anti-Nazi resisters.

Throughout history, women have had innumerable opportunities to appear as if whatever they were doing was totally appropriate for their seemingly weak and docile role in society. Because women had for so long been relegated to a secondary status, it was easy for male Nazis to think that women were incapable of committing acts of defiance. Women exploited this bias by pretending to be silly, or weak and simple-minded as they carried out daring acts of sabotage . . . often right under the noses of the Germans. Women could often incorporate resistance work into their routine activities as daughters, sisters, mothers, and wives. Laundry baskets could also include secret documents, medical supplies, and food ration cards. A seemingly simple-minded old woman would not be suspected of coordinating the transmission of coded intelligence to the partisans and the Allies. A handicapped and hard-of-hearing female apartment manager couldn't possibly be hiding thirty Jews in the basement. How could there be anything more than a baby in that carriage? And if a Jewish woman was blonde and blue-eyed, she had even more options to resist because she could pass as a Gentile. Sometimes a fragile looking girl on a train, who appeared to need help lifting a suitcase (full of illegal documents), could gain assistance from a big, strong and gallant German.

The youngest of the female resisters, some as young as twelve, were born between 1915 and 1921. With few exceptions, as children, they were used to being protected and obeying authorities. While some of the older teenagers might have been more independent and adventurous, most were still bound by their culture's traditional belief that good girls stayed home and helped their families until they were married. Following marriage, they would make a home with their husbands, and take care of their own families. There were, however, a few independent girls, sometimes to the dismay of their traditional families, who ventured out of their homes, and explored the world beyond their immediate community. And there were some girls who came from more sophisticated families, and who were encouraged to pursue a higher education and profession.

Some of these professional women were extremely effective in the resistance. Many were married to men who were prominent in government and the military, and had the social, professional, and financial connections that housewives lacked. Because of their greater visibility, however, these women also took on great risk when defying the Nazis. Both Gentile and Jewish (until they were prohibited from working) female teachers, social workers, doctors, dentists, and lawyers interacted with students, patients, and clients on a daily basis. Teachers, for example, participated in early resistance activities by providing places for people to exchange messages, and organized escape strategies for their students and their families. Doctors and dentists helped by continuing to serve their Jewish patients, as well as secretly obtaining and storing medications and medical equipment. Attorneys drew up legal documents that helped Jews obtain false citizenship papers and new identities. The Gentile female professionals who helped Jews also refrained from denouncing those who they knew were passing as Gentiles. Professional women also used their connections to find hiding places and provide emergency health care. Both Jewish and Gentile female professionals were particularly important in partisan groups. For example, Catholic aristocrat Irena Adamowicz (1910–1973), was an administrator of the Catholic Girl Scout movement who helped the Zionist group, *Hashomer Ha-Tsa'ir*.[22] As a courier for the Polish Underground Army, she also helped Jews.

While many resistance activities could be incorporated into women's daily household and professional routines, there were others that were both far from routine, and even more dangerous. One of these involved the rescue and subsequent care of both the Polish and Allied airmen and soldiers. Since

---

22. The *Hashomer Ha-Tsa'ir-Halutz* (Pioneers) is an active, highly organized, socialist youth movement which originated in the Galicia region of the Austro-Hungarian Empire, and spread throughout Europe. Initially, its members were trained for immigration to, and life in, Palestine, the Hebrew homeland. In 1948, this is where Israel would be established as an independent Jewish state. With approximately 100,000 members, they were very active in anti-German resistance.

it was easier for women than men to move around the countryside, they were able to gather and communicate vital information about German locations and military strength. They were also able to scout areas where Allied airplanes were supposed to be landing, or parachuting men and supplies. Women took great risks to find these men and supplies, and then get them where they needed to go. Women would also hide, feed, and nurse injured airmen who had been shot down, and then help them escape.

Another highly dangerous resistance activity that often fell to the women was finding safe houses for Jews, especially Jewish children. First, the head of a Gentile home or farm had to be determined to be reliable, willing, and able to house Jews. Next, the Jews had to be found and convinced to go to a safe house, or to let their children go. Then, it was necessary to secretly transport the terrified Jews to the new hiding place. Resistance workers also had to provide the necessary food and medicines to keep these hidden Jews alive. If neighbors became suspicious, or bounty hunters appeared, the Jews had to be immediately moved to a new hiding place. Sometimes they even escorted Jews over mountains, through forests, and across borders. Who could have imagined that these clandestine and perilous resistance activities were taking place in modern times?

Post-World War I Poland was modernizing, and for many young women, it was a unique time when the future of their country and their personal lives looked bright. Their country was now democratic, eager for its people to recover from the war, and to become vibrant and successful. Women had obtained the right to vote at the end of World War I, and some became very active in politics. Their many political activities provided training as leaders, as well as an organized foundation and network for their eventual anti-Nazi resistance. Furthermore, the many technological advances of the early 1900s—including improvements in automobiles, radios, plastic, and nylon—made women's lives easier, gave them more mobility, and allowed them more time for endeavors outside of the home. Emerging industries also provided large numbers of new types of jobs, so even more women left the countryside to work and live in cities. As women became more exposed to the outside world, their perspectives broadened, and their roles expanded.

While the lives of urbanized women changed dramatically, the lives of rural women remained, for the most part, unchanged. The growing dissimilarity between urban and rural lifestyles would also provide significant differences in the ways women would resist the coming German occupation. Urban Jewish women were generally more educated, sophisticated, and worldly, so they were better prepared to understand, communicate, and fit in with the Gentiles. Thus, it was easier for them to pass as Gentiles. Their professional ties and friendships with Gentiles would benefit them when they needed help with the resistance, or when they needed a safe place to hide. Rural Jewish women, on the other hand, were usually traditional rather than modern in their thoughts, appearance, and behavior. They were isolated, less educated, and not familiar with Gentiles. They did not have the same opportunities to develop friendships with non-Jews, so it was extremely difficult for them to engage in resistance activities. Lacking money as well as the linguistic and social skills of urban women, it was next to impossible for them to pass as Gentiles, and just as difficult to find places to hide. Another factor determining women's options to resist the Nazis would be whether they lived in the German or Soviet sectors of Poland. Since western Poland had been occupied first, there had been no time to plan resistance strategies. Some women in the eastern Soviet-occupied sector, however, had already seen what the Germans had done, and had no doubt about what was coming their way.

Faced with discrimination, impossibly crowded and squalid living conditions, starvation, disease, and the prospect of death at every turn, Polish Gentile and Jewish women were determined to protect their loved ones to the best of their abilities. As Jewish husbands, sons, and fathers (many of whom were decorated veterans of World War I) were beaten and murdered, or arrested and deported to certain death in the camps, traditional gender roles changed, placing greater responsibilities upon women both within their families and within their communities. Many Polish Gentile women, whose fathers, brothers, husbands, and sons had also fought in World War I, and were now being conscripted into the German military, were similarly alone. They also faced poverty and hunger, and risked death every time they helped a Jew. Whether Gentile or Jewish, these women were constantly responsible for making life and death decisions.

With few, if any, resources, and so little hope, why did some of these women, unlike so many others, choose to defy oppression? Despite their many differences, what qualities did they share that compelled them to fight? Did any survive? If so, what happened to them after the war? After talking with them, it became clear that whether rich or poor, rural or urban, these remarkable women did not see themselves as heroines. Instead, they each insist that they were just ordinary people who, when confronted with the senseless Nazi horror, just did the only thing that made any sense: they did the right thing. And seventy-plus years later, as their stories reveal, they have never stopped "doing the right thing."

What follows are the unforgettable stories of four young Jewish females who had been living normal lives until the Nazis changed their world forever. Three were teenagers. The fourth was a little girl. While each of their experiences was unique, there were certain important qualities and circumstances that they shared. Of primary importance to the survival of each of these remarkable young women was the fact that at important points along the way, they were helped by Polish Gentiles. Each woman felt it was important that the actions of these Gentiles be included in their story. What follows first is the story of Manya Feldman, the nurse, fighter, and "crazy Jewess." Second is Faye Schulman, the nurse, fighter, and photographer. Third is Lola Lieber, the artist and forger-on-the-run, who passed as a Gentile. Finally, there is Miriam Brysk, the little girl who dressed liked a boy and carried a gun.

Jewish Partisan Activity 1942–1944

"I only survived because of my youth and plain good luck."

Chapter 3

Manya Barman Auster Feldman

1923, Dombrovitsa, Poland—West Bloomfield, Michigan

Manya Barman
West Berlin, Germany 1946

Manya Feldman
West Bloomfield, Michigan 2012

E legantly attired, with her thick, impeccably styled strawberry-blond hair providing a chic frame for her youthful face, Manya Feldman sat gracefully on the shaded veranda of the Fleischman Residence in West Bloomfield, Michigan. From her appearance, the last thing anyone would have imagined or believed is that 74 years ago, this lovely woman was a tough teenage partisan, fighting Germans in the dense Polish forests.

Ever alert, she quickly spotted my car entering the parking lot. I caught her eye and waved, and realized, even before I met her, that she still exhibited many of the qualities that had served her so well during her time as a young Polish-Jewish partisan during World War II. Seemingly calm and cool despite the 95 degrees and 95% humidity of a Michigan July, she was ready to talk with a total stranger about deeply personal, and searingly painful experiences.

Greeting me with a warm hug, she was immediately concerned about my needs: Did I have any trouble finding her residence? Was I thirsty? Too hot? Too cold in the air-conditioning? At 89 years of age, she was the perfect hostess—treating me as if I were the important person instead of it being the other way around. She was charming. She was competent. She was confident. And she was in charge. And if we had been surrounded by Germans in a frigid Polish forest in the middle of the night, she definitely was the one I'd want to follow.

In fact, I was already following her. Briskly pushing her walker and its small attached oxygen tank, she led me through the bustling lobby en route to a private meeting room. With her eyes constantly scanning our surroundings, she never missed a detail, stopping every few feet to make an introduction, or to indicate a point of interest—a lovely piece of art, a lively bird habitat, a notice for an upcoming art exhibit. Finally seated, and assured that I was comfortable, and just as if we were having a routine conversation, she began her story. Within a few sentences, the clean, well-equipped, modern building in which we comfortably sat—as well as almost three-quarters of a century—evaporated. In its place was a dark, cold room in a primitive and brutally overcrowded ghetto. And I was listening to the voice of a terrified and confused Jewish teenager whose life was about to change forever.

The next three years would take Manya through horrors that still defy the imagination, as she learned to live, to fight, and to survive along with the Soviet partisans in the dense and swampy forests of Poland. And as her story continued, I began to hear the strong voice of a heroic young woman who made heartrending decisions on a moment's notice faced death on a daily basis, and overcame overwhelming dangers—eventually surviving events that for far too many others, had been unsurvivable.

Here is Manya's story . . .

West Bloomfield, Michigan, 2012

I was born in 1923, and grew up in Dombrovitsa, a city in the eastern part of what was then Poland, not far from the Russian border. The closest big city was Pinsk, which is now in Belarus. Approximately 3,000 of Dombrovitsa's 5,000 residents were Orthodox Jews, who were very poor. In our immediate family, there were five children: four daughters and a son. Our extended family was huge: close to 200. Of those, only three of us, first cousins, survived the war. And of these three, I am the only one still living.

My father had been wounded when he fought for the Czar in the Russian Army during World War I, and as a result, his four fingers on one hand had been amputated. After the war, since he couldn't do heavy manual labor, people looked down on him for being handicapped. He was an industrious man, however, and determined to provide for his family, so he went into the grocery business and opened a small market. Both of my parents worked hard at the market, and even though we weren't rich, we were considered to be middle-class. My parents were very loving, and their greatest goal was for us children to become educated. We adored our parents and worked hard to please them. We didn't have much, but we had our family, our religion, our clubs, and cultural organizations. Looking back, I think that having had a happy childhood gave me strength to overcome the difficulties that came later.

As an Orthodox Jewish family, we eagerly looked forward to our joyful Friday night *Shabbos* (Sabbath) dinners, which we always shared with those who were less fortunate. We had a very lively family, and enjoyed laughing and singing the traditional songs. We must have made quite a commotion, because sometimes Gentiles who lived nearby would stop and watch our celebration through the window. While this might seem strange now, we never acknowledged their presence or said anything to them. Our interactions with Gentiles never developed into more than "hello" and "goodbye." Outside of our safe Jewish community, we were subjected to a lot of anti-Semitism. Gentiles would call us names, shout terrible insults, and sometimes throw rocks at us when they saw us on the streets. There was often anti-Jewish graffiti on the walls of Jewish homes and businesses, and Jewish stores were sometimes picketed and boycotted. We were also subjected to many legal restrictions, including the ability of Jews to go to public schools, universities, or have professional careers. So whenever possible, we stayed away from the Gentiles. We lived right next to each other, but in completely separate worlds.

Inside the Jewish community, our lives were peaceful and happy. We were well-educated at our own Jewish schools by Jewish teachers. In addition to our Hebrew education, we were fortunate that we learned Polish history, geography, customs, and how to speak and write the Polish language. That way, if necessary, we could fit in with our surroundings. Little did I know that this knowledge would soon help keep me alive. Other Jews, who lived in communities where they learned nothing about the Polish culture or language, would not be so lucky.

Even as a young child, I was always very active, always a "doer." I wanted to be involved in my parents' store rather than spend my time at home, sewing and keeping house. My parents trusted me, and gave me a lot of responsibilities. As a matter of fact, when I was only eight years old, I was the one who went early to open the store. This was because my father had to go to *Shul* (a Jewish house of worship) in the mornings, while my mother was busy with my sisters and brother. I would wait at the store until my father or mother came, and then I would go to Hebrew School. After school, I'd go back to work in the store. When I finally got home, ate dinner, and finished my homework, there still was plenty of housework and gardening to do, so I was always busy.

Other than the one Jewish doctor, there were very few Jewish professionals in our city. Our little store did alright because even though our Gentile customers were anti-Semitic and rude to us, there wasn't anywhere else for them to shop. On Christmas and Easter, however, the store was closed. On those days, we had to stay shut up in our house. We didn't dare go outside, because the Gentiles were even more hostile than usual toward Jews on these holidays. In their churches, their priests told them that the Jews had killed

Jesus, so after their services, they would be riled up and come out ready to kill any Jew that they could find. We always had to be careful, but we understood the "rules" and knew how to live with them.

Our village didn't have a Jewish high school, so when the time came, those few parents who could afford it, would send their children to live and continue their education in bigger towns. I wanted more than anything to be able to go to high school. Despite my endless tearful and bitter begging, however, it wasn't possible because it was too expensive. My father had four daughters, and at that time, getting them married was considered much more important than getting them educated. So when my older sister finished elementary school, she became a seamstress. When I finished, I went to work in our store. Since boys were expected to marry and support their own families, however, it was important for my older brother to learn a well-paying skill. So the plan for him when he finished school was to train to become a watchmaker.

Even in the midst of these challenges, we didn't feel particularly threatened. Our Jewish culture had evolved over centuries within unfriendly environments, and we knew how to create a sense of warmth and security for ourselves. There were several Zionist groups in town, some of which were very religious, believing that God would protect and save them. Other Zionist groups were totally secular (non-religious), and believed that Jews would have to work, and even fight if necessary, to get to *Palestine*.[23] These well-organized groups, with their large number of members and good leaders, would later provide strong networks for anti-Nazi resistance activities. As teenagers, we belonged to the *Hashomer Ha-Tsa'ir-Halutz*. We had meetings, sang songs, and read a lot of literature. We talked about the Zionist movement, and instilled in the younger children the desire to go to Palestine. That was our dream, and the dream of our parents.

In August 1939, when I was sixteen, something important happened that we didn't know about. And even if we had known about it, we wouldn't have understood it: the Germans and the Soviets made a secret agreement that they would soon split Poland between them. A week later, the Germans

---

23. Considered by Jews to be their homeland, *Palestine* is an ancient region in the Middle East between the Mediterranean Sea and the Jordan River that has historically been the center of territorial disputes, as well as government and boundary changes.

invaded and occupied western and much of central Poland. Then, two weeks later, the Soviets invaded and occupied eastern Poland. So the country of Poland disappeared. Just like that. No more Poland. Our village was suddenly under Soviet Communist rule. And although life became very hard, we considered ourselves fortunate because since we lived in what was now the Soviet sector, we weren't targeted for extermination. The Russians closed the Jewish schools, but they allowed the Jewish children to go to the Russian public school, which was very good. Jews were still allowed to work and live in their own homes, although under communism, Jewish-owned businesses were taken over by the government, or "socialized." We could manage to survive as long as we were careful, and stayed in our own little world—far away from the Gentiles.

Throughout history, the Jewish people had survived oppressions by adapting to the conditions that were imposed upon them. So we felt we would survive as long as we could adapt to what was happening. Tragically, we believed it was temporary. How could it not be temporary? Once we adjusted, we even felt lucky. The Soviets were better than the anti-Semitic Poles. And anyone was better than the Germans. Although it must have been difficult for our parents, we innocent children were happy. And so during the almost two years that we were under the Soviet Occupation, we were spared the horrors of Nazi Germany, never imagining what was to come.

In a surprise attack, on June 22, 1941, the Germans broke their pact with the Soviets. Suddenly, instead of being their allies, the Soviets had become the victims of the Germans, and many were massacred or taken to prison of war (POW) camps where they were brutalized and starved. So on a lovely, but eerie, Sunday morning, while we sat together on our front porch, our lives changed forever. Amidst the sunshine, soft breezes, and the cheerful sounds of singing birds, we heard the rumbling and felt the vibrations of the Germans before we saw them. We didn't understand what was happening. How could we? Suddenly, as if they had been dropped down from the sky, the Germans came roaring down our street on motorcycles followed by huge tanks. We just continued sitting on our porch, petrified. Completely quiet, barely breathing. And then, as if it hadn't happened, the Germans were gone. In fact, it was easier to believe it actually hadn't happened than to comprehend what it meant.

Soon enough, we could hear the joyous crowds of Polish Gentiles welcoming their heroic "liberators" with shouts of thanks, songs of welcome, and bouquets of flowers. They were grateful that the Germans had gotten rid of the despised Soviets, who had oppressed Poland for centuries. We Jews certainly didn't show any enthusiasm for the Germans' arrival. We knew all too well what had happened to the Jews in Nazi Germany, starting in 1933, in Austria and Czechoslovakia in 1938, and since 1939, in western Poland. Soon, we were in for another shock, when our Polish neighbors, taking their cues from the Germans, quickly started screaming at us, "Now it's going to be your end. Now you will die!" It was utter chaos. And we watched and listened in utter disbelief and sorrow.

Next, while we were still trying to comprehend what was going on, a truly terrible thing happened. Two men, who for years had done business with my father, came and grabbed him from our porch, hitting and shaking him and shouting, "Come with us, you dirty Jew!" Shocked and terrified, Papa tried to keep his voice steady so we wouldn't worry, and asked, "Where are you taking me? What's happening?" They handled him roughly, and ordered him to shut his mouth, saying, "You'll find out soon enough. Dirty Jew." Unable to believe our eyes, we watched them drag Papa away. One minute our family was sitting together talking on our front porch, and the next minute our beloved father was being dragged away in a riot. My brother somehow had the presence of mind to run inside the house and hide in the attic. The rest of us followed quickly, closing the doors and shutters behind us. We didn't know what was going on, so how could we know what to do? What was happening to our father? What was happening to our world? The unknown was unbearable.

In the stuffy, hot attic, we sat together in bewildered silence. After a couple of hours, my mother and I couldn't take it anymore so we decided to go and see what was happening. As we ran through the town, we saw that we weren't alone. The terrified mothers, sisters, wives, and daughters of other prisoners were also running to the town square. When we got there, we couldn't believe our eyes. The Germans had taken 200 middle-aged Jewish men, forced them to sit on the ground, and pointed machine guns at their heads, ready to shoot for any—or even no—reason. We saw my father among them. We felt as if we would explode from the helplessness. Then, my mother and I, along with all the women whose husbands, fathers, and brothers had been taken, ran to the mayor and to the priest to beg them to help us. Hundreds of women crying, "*Please! Do something for us.*"

This call for help, this spontaneous and desperate act of resistance, infuriated the Germans, who then felt compelled to show that they would not tolerate any rebellion. So they grabbed the Jewish prisoners, and accused them of being communists, screaming, "This is what happens in a communistic town . . . these are all communists and now we're going to get rid of the whole group." Finally responding to the women's agonized begging, the priest and the mayor came to the Germans and said, "Yes, there might be a few communists in town, but these men are all good Jews." Eventually, towards the evening, the Germans released all but twenty-two of the men, who'd been picked at random to be used as hostages. The rest of them, including my father, were sent home. The Germans announced that if anything happened to any German soldier, the hostages would be executed.

Once again, we tried to adapt to these new authorities, hoping that we could outlast whatever they intended to do. For a while, until the ghetto was established, we still lived in our own homes, but we were continuously subjected to terrible new laws. For example, since the sidewalks were for Gentiles, who were considered to be "humans," Jews, who were "non-humans," had to walk in the streets with the horses. Jews couldn't own a store or any kind of business. Jews couldn't have any livestock, and since we'd all had our own geese and cows, this was the first step toward starvation. Then Jews had to relinquish all their furs, silver, gold—whatever was valuable. Within two weeks, a *Judenrat,* consisting of Jewish men who'd been selected by the Germans, was established to keep the Jews under control.

The situation was becoming impossible. We were deprived of food, of all personal freedom, of everything. One day, the Germans announced that they were granting the Gentile population complete freedom, telling them that they could go and loot and steal whatever they wanted from the Jewish homes. And that's just what they did. They went on a violent looting rampage, making it obvious that the Jews of Dombrovitsa would not be able to survive by *adjusting* to the Germans. Since their only goal was for us to die, what was there to adjust to? The only way to survive was to try to escape. But where could we go?

By the third month of the Occupation, a ghetto was formed, and the Jews were forced to leave their homes and move to an overcrowded area that was roped off from the rest of the town. There was no actual wall, they just roped off two streets, and put in a single guarded-gate entrance so we couldn't go out or go in.* The windows of the houses that faced outside the ghetto were boarded up so we "non-humans" couldn't see where the *real* human beings lived. The *Judenrat*, under Gestapo orders, was now in charge of the ghetto. Every Jew was counted and registered. If someone escaped, others would be punished or even killed. In this way, they made us responsible for each other. We had an understanding, "I'll see to it that you can't escape so that nothing will happen to us." Resistance would mean hurting our own people. They used us against each other, and therefore against ourselves.

We all had to wear yellow Stars of David sewn onto the front and back of our clothes. Our family was put into a house along with two other families—thirteen people. There was a living room, a small bedroom, and a kitchen. So we lived in one room, one family lived in another room, and the other family lived in the kitchen. There were no telephones, no beds. We slept on the floor. Sanitary conditions were disgusting—instead of indoor plumbing, we used filthy, foul-smelling outhouses. Instead of clean indoor running water, we used outdoor wells. Food rations were so limited that we were starving, and in the streets we could see people—friends, neighbors— dying of starvation, dysentery, and typhoid. Still, in spite of the misery in the ghetto, we tried to make it seem as normal as possible. A little black market soon developed. Gentiles would come to the fence, and if we had anything they needed, they would give us food in exchange. Maybe we'd get a scrawny chicken for a gold wedding ring. Or a loaf of bread for some salt or tobacco. Since our family had managed to smuggle in some merchandise from our store, we were able to make trades for a while. Jews also created secret make-shift schools and synagogues. We managed to celebrate the holidays. Some resemblance to Jewish life went on no matter what the circumstances. We were determined not to lose our humanity, so we resisted dehumanization in whatever little ways we could.

---

*Note: *Years later, I often spoke to schools and other groups, and the same question would always come up, "Why didn't you escape?" You know why? Because we were surrounded. It wasn't just by the German-occupation. We were surrounded by enemies who were all too willing to help the Germans. I'd say that about seventy–eighty percent of the Gentiles were in tune with the Germans. Even if we got out, there was nowhere for us to go and almost nowhere that we could hide. Wherever we went, we were immediately recognized as Jews because our clothes were so different from the Gentiles. And during the liquidation of the ghetto, Gentiles were promised for each Jew they found, they'd get a kilogram of soap or a kilogram of sugar. So they caught Jews left and right.*

The Germans forced everybody to go to work at hard, physical labor. It didn't matter what it was, just as long as we worked, and worked hard. It was day-to-day living, we just worked and prayed to live one more day. In the wintertime, we cleaned snow off the streets and railway tracks. If the Germans felt like it, they would give us old toothbrushes and make us clean the sidewalks. In the summer, we dragged all kinds of construction materials to the bridges that were being built, or we worked in the fields. At that time, I was running the threshing machine in the fields. It was hot and dirty, and the dust made it a struggle to breathe or even see clearly. It was a miserable way to spend eight hours a day.

One morning, I don't know what got into me, but I just decided not to go to work. I knew I was taking a terrible risk, but I just couldn't face another day in that field. Looking back, I guess that this was my first individual act of deliberate resistance, but of course, I didn't know it then. That night, the Germans asked the *Judenrat* to give them a list of the people who hadn't reported to work that day. I was arrested and taken to Gestapo headquarters. Much to my surprise, it turned out that there were several of us: men, boys, women, and girls, who had all been arrested and taken to headquarters. We sat there all night and saw and heard horrible things. In front of us, two Germans beat a Polish Gentile man so badly with rubber pipes that he was bleeding from every part of his body. Then they took him out and they shot him. They screamed at us, "You see what's going to happen if you don't follow orders!" This was their way of killing our thoughts of resistance.

Unknown to me, and in spite of the danger, my father, brother, and eldest sister had been discussing ways to save our family. The only option was to escape to the forest and try to live there. Of course, they had no idea what would happen in the forest, or if they could live long enough to even *get* to the forest. So they decided that the family would have to split up, that way, hopefully, someone from the family would survive. My father, brother, and older sister decided that since they were the strongest, that they would go first. If they survived and established a place in the forest where we could all live, they would then come back for my mother, my little two sisters, and me. They had already packed small knapsacks and were ready to go to the forest at a moment's notice. Our neighbor and his two sons would join them. All that they waited for now was the right moment to escape. Until then, our days continued as usual.

One day when I was at work at a construction site, the authorities told us that we didn't have to come to work the next day. That was very strange. So we knew it was going to be the end. As we slowly returned to our ghetto "homes," we had no idea what to do. How do you think about—how can you endure something like this, knowing that tomorrow you and your family—everyone you know is going to be killed? That night at bedtime, our father told us to put on a couple of dresses along with our pajamas, and go to sleep. Despite my terror, I did somehow fall asleep. At about midnight—out of nowhere—there was a soft knock on our window. It was our neighbor, who told Papa, "Do you know the ghetto is surrounded? Jews are trying to run into the forest! There are already many dead . . . the Germans are shooting everyone! We need to run—*NOW!*" By then, I was out of bed and standing nearby, watching what was going on. My father, brother, and sister rushed around with strange expressions on their faces. My mother stood by silently, holding on to my two small sisters. Even though I saw what was happening, I couldn't comprehend that my father and brother were about to leave us. I was soon stunned to see that my older sister, who I really looked up to, was also getting ready to go.

I asked her, "You mean to tell me you're going?" She said, "Yes, I'm going." "You mean to tell me you're going to leave mother?" She didn't answer. But for a short moment, she looked me straight in the eye . . . and then she didn't even glance at me again. As I stood there watching in absolute bewilderment, I tried to make sense of what was going on. And I tried to decide what would be the best thing for me to do. Should I stay and help my mother and the little ones? Or should I go with my father? This is a decision that no one should have to make. How could I leave my mother? Ultimately, however, I decided, that if my older sister was going, then I was going, too. So in agony, I chose to go with my father. And, in a rush, we left. My mother didn't say a word. We left her and the two sweet little girls . . . just standing there. Our hope was that they would somehow be safe in the ghetto. But we never saw them again.

So there were seven of us that night: my sister, my brother, my father, me, and the neighbor with his two boys. We walked to an unguarded ghetto gate and quietly slipped out and proceeded down the street, all the way out of town to the river. We spotted a little canoe, and in two shifts, we crossed the river. On the other side, we ran to a Gentile village where the mayor had been a customer of my father's. We knew that he was a good man, so we headed to his house. My father told him that the ghetto was surrounded and the Jews were being killed. So at great risk to himself and his family, the man offered to find us a place to hide. We couldn't stay at his house because he was the head of the village, and Germans came there often. So he put us up in bushes not far from another river, where we sat for hours, wondering what would happen next.

Towards the afternoon, his son came and gave us some food, and told us that the ghettos were being liquidated. He said that the Jews from neighboring cities had all been taken on trains to the town of Sarny, where mass "graves," meaning vast, shallow pits, had already been prepared for them. "Don't stay here. Go—do what you have to do," he urged us. From our hiding place we could hear the trains going by. We could also hear the constant pops as the Germans shot Jews who were jumping from the trains. We knew we had to go. So we got up and headed further into the forest. I would learn much later that my mother and precious little sisters were among the fifteen thousand innocent Jews that were rounded up and sent to Sarny to be "liquidated" during that hideous week in August 1942. To this day, I have never lost the vision of them standing there. I think of it all the time. I see them in front of me, my mother silent, my sisters confused and crying. I feel so guilty for leaving them. Guilty for living, when they died. I am now eighty-nine years old, and the memory still haunts me.

We didn't have equipment or skills for living in the forest, but we soon learned how to scavenge for edible roots and berries. We also learned to disregard our usual respect for honesty, in order to steal potatoes, often rotten, from nearby farms. We learned how to sleep on the frozen ground in the winter, and in the insect and disease-infested mud in the summer. Constantly on the move to avoid discovery, we hid in fields, small villages, and sometimes with various groups in the forest. At one point, we were spotted by a bounty hunter, who would have turned us in for a reward. So we raced deeper into the forest. Anti-Semitism was so strong where we were that many Gentiles would have killed Jews with their own bare hands, even without a reward. Since they had been taught that we were "Christ-Killers," they considered it a good deed to kill a Jew. If they hadn't assisted the Germans the way they did, thousands and thousands of Jews would have been saved.

Our first November in the forest, we were living in a little bunker that my father and brother had built out of rocks and branches. But when the snows began, we were afraid that we'd leave tracks that the Germans could follow. We would only be safe if we could get out of the snow. It turned out that there were some good people not too far away. They were Seventh Day Adventists,[24] who are committed to nonviolence. So my father took me and my sister to them and we held our breath as he asked them politely if they could keep us during the wintertime. We were so relieved when they said they would take me, and they would also find another family to take my sister. These people, without any notice, risked their lives, to open their homes and hearts to desperate strangers. They made us feel welcome even though we came from such a different world. And we did our best to help them in every way possible. Once, my host family questioned the Jewish belief in a God that would single them out for such horror. When they mentioned the possibility of my converting to Adventism, I said, "Oh, no. I was born a Jew and I'll die a Jew." To this day, I am so grateful that there were some Gentiles, unlike so many others, who risked their lives to help Jews. They were true heroes.

During that time, we'd been hearing rumors about fierce partisan fighting groups that were being established in the forests. They were organized by Soviet soldiers who'd escaped from brutal German prisoner of war camps, where they'd been dying like flies. Determined to fight the Germans in any way they could, they formed their own combat units. They soon realized, however, that partisan fighting was different from the traditional military fighting for which they'd been trained. Now they would be fighting the Germans from the *back* instead of the front lines, as they had in the military. Since they didn't have enough supplies and weapons, they had to raid villages and farms to get what they needed. When the partisans were eventually able to make contact with their government's headquarters in Moscow, the government started sending important information, food, medicines, supplies, and weapons to the forest. They also sent a highly trained military man to lead them.

---

24. The *Seventh Day Adventist Church* is a Protestant denomination of Christianity that began in the United States in the 1860s, and then spread to Europe. *Adventists* observe the Sabbath on Saturday instead of Sunday, are very health conscious, and believe in religious freedom.

His name was Sydir Kovpak (1887–1967), and I learned later that he had been a famous Russian military hero, personally decorated in World War I by the Russian Czar Nicholas II.[25] Following the Russian Revolution, he had joined the Russian Communist Party, then joined the Red Army, and fought against the Germans. In addition to his other skills, he was also a master of *guerilla*[26] war tactics. The Soviets parachuted him down into the forest one night, and he then proceeded to find, organize, and train his own group of partisans. This was a very tricky operation in the middle of the swampy forest. Word of these partisan activities spread, and little by little, the Kovpaks were joined by other escaping Soviet soldiers, as well as some Jews, and even some Ukrainians and Poles, who were also running from the Germans.

At this time, the Kovpak *Otriad* (Russian for a "group apart" or "on its own") was stationed only around twenty kilometers from where we were, and they were scouting Jews, and even local Polish people to join them. A few weeks after my sister and I had moved in with the Seventh Day Adventists, my father was approached by a Kovpak scout, and he decided that we should join them. He felt very strongly that even though we probably wouldn't survive, that at least we could kill some Germans. We wouldn't accept our fate passively. We would avenge the deaths of our murdered family. So he took my sister and me from the Seventh Day Adventists, and we went into the forest to search for these partisans. At that time, I was sorry to leave the family that had sheltered us. I felt my sister and I would be safer in the village than in the forest, especially in the winter.

My father, however, had become committed to doing whatever was necessary to fight the Germans. So we said our sad goodbyes, wished our kind "families" well, promising to contact them when the world was safe again. At that point, leaving a warm house with food to eat and going to the cold forest with only occasional food, didn't make me feel lucky. To our shock and sorrow, we learned much later that their entire village had been destroyed soon after we'd left . . . no one was left alive. I was haunted by the feeling that it

25. Russia's *Czar Nicholas II* was the last Emperor of Russia, ruling from November 1894 until his enforced abdication in March 1917.

26. *Guerrilla* is a Spanish word meaning "little war," and refers to individual or small group fights, raids, and ambushes that are often utilized by civilians when rebelling against an oppressor.

Manya Barman
Poland, 1943

might have been our fault. That maybe someone had found out about us and denounced our host families to the Germans. And that because of us, the innocent villagers had been obliterated in retaliation.

After walking for what seemed like forever, but actually was only one long night in the cold forest, we finally got to the Kovpak headquarters. I don't know what I was expecting, but I was definitely surprised by what I saw. It was a complete community of different kinds of people—all busy—and totally hidden in the forest. From inexperienced teenagers, to farmers, to military heroes, this determined and disciplined group would create many serious problems for the Germans. While the partisans knew they would never actually defeat the Germans, their goal was to inflict as much damage as possible. And they did. In fact, the Germans hated and feared them.

Upon our arrival, the first thing they told us was, "You know this is a partisan movement, so families don't exist here. There are no families. We have to separate you. Wherever you'll be told to go, that's where you go." Thus began our partisan training. There were five battalions, each with one thousand members, scattered throughout the area. Each had a leader who got his commands from their headquarters. Each headquarters communicated by radio with the Soviets in Moscow. My father and my brother were assigned one battalion, and my sister and I went to another. My father worked so hard. He felt badly that he couldn't be a fighter because of his hand, so he gladly took on all kinds of chores. My brother, who was nineteen, soon became a regular combat soldier. My sister and I stayed in Battalion #1, which was responsible for domestic work like food preparation and laundry. We started in the laundry, but eventually, I became a nurse, and my sister went to another battalion, where she became a combat fighter with a rifle.

In the laundry, there was no soap, so I used ashes instead. Ashes contain lye, which creates an extremely harsh laundry cleaner. I washed the clothes in water I'd heated to boiling on the fire. The partisans' clothes were very heavy, heavier than canvas, and very rough, like burlap. It was a horrible job, my hands were always bloody and running with sores, but I was very diligent. I did my work, and didn't complain. I knew that what the others had to do was much worse. Fortunately, the guys that were in charge liked me and decided to "promote" me to kitchen duty. So no more laundry. But then I got up at four in the morning to work with whatever food was available. For a while, there was meat from stolen cows, and small, wild animals, as well as potatoes, and bread. We ate our meals, and afterwards, when possible, we even sang, danced, and told stories. Many of us had been in Zionist clubs and knew the same Zionist songs. It might seem weird, but in spite of our circumstances, we were still young people, and did what we could to keep our spirits up.

We were often on the move because the Germans were always on our tails. We stayed a few days, sometimes even a week, in one place, until we had to run again from the Germans. We were constantly on the go, just moving around and doing all kinds of damage to the German Army. Since our partisan group had been established and supported by the Soviets, its primary goal was to protect their own country from the Germans, who were advancing into the Soviet Union. So the Kovpaks were like a grassroots branch of the Soviet military. They weren't particularly interested in the problems of local people. And they weren't interested in the problems of the Jews. They had a job to do, and although there was some anti-Semitism, as long as we helped them, they let us stay.

Despite the challenges, the partisans were amazing fighters and a tremendous hindrance to the Germans. They went out and found German installations and destroyed them, bringing back whatever supplies, food, medicines, blankets, and clothing they could carry. It was not unusual to see a partisan wearing German clothes, which made it hard to know who was who! One of their major goals was to prevent the Germans from transporting troops, weapons, and supplies to the front. Partisans shot up German trains, ripped up train tracks, and also used dynamite to blow up the train cars, tracks, and bridges. Our group often participated in armed combat, inflicting heavy casualties on the Germans, always taking their weapons, and whatever else would be useful back to the group. During that time, my primary responsibility was to be a nurse. I worked hard assisting a doctor who was part of our group, and learned how to take care of wounds and sickness.

Partisans also communicated crucial information about the Germans to other partisans and to the Soviet government. Today, even senior citizens have cell phones, and use the internet, so it's hard to imagine communicating without our modern technology. But back then, some of the forest partisan headquarters did have access to radio communication with their government in Moscow, but otherwise, the partisans had only the most primitive means of communication, such as using couriers to carry information, money, and medications from group to group. Our "runners" raced through the forests and villages carrying important news and secret information about both partisan and German activities. Sometimes the information was written in code. Sometimes it was memorized, also in code.

Getting supplies was of paramount importance. Of course, the partisans couldn't go into a city to buy what they needed. Sometimes it was parachuted down to us, but since we were always on the move, and the forest made it hard for pilots to find good places to drop the supplies, we usually had to steal what we needed from nearby villages and farms. The inhabitants of the villages had to go along with what we said, because we were tough, and had weapons, just like a regular army. There was a chain of command and everyone followed orders . . . *or else*.

I can't overemphasize how important it was to get a hold of any kind of weapon—a knife, a pistol, a hunting rifle, any rifle—and the materials for making explosives. These weren't just to fight the Germans or unfriendly peasants and bounty hunters, but also to protect ourselves and each other. We each knew that if we were captured, that we had to try to kill ourselves. Otherwise, when we were tortured, we might give up information that could damage our cause, and endanger others. So, in addition to learning how to be a nurse, I also learned how to be an effective fighter—in one-on-one combat, as well as in blowing up trucks, train tracks, and bridges.

In addition to weapons, it was also crucial that we have access to water. When we could, we carried it with us. Other times, if we were lucky, there would be a river or stream nearby. If not, we had to break through the ice, or dig for it in the marshy land. The forest was filled with swamps, but if untreated, that disease-infected water would make us sick. While on the run, we often had to dig holes for water, which would be black and thick, just like coffee. And it was filled with who knows what? Insects, disease. Some people ended up dying from the water. Every hour, every day, we were constantly under the strain that we were going to starve to death. Or die of hideous diseases . . . or get caught . . . get tortured . . . get killed. There was never any relief from this. All we thought about was just living through that hour. Just living through that day. And for more than two years, while I lived in the forest as a partisan, sleeping in teepees, sleeping on the ground, in holes in the ground, the whole time, I never took off my dress. It had become a part of me.

The winter of 1943 was especially harsh. By then, I'd been promoted to being a nurse, and was responsible for the sick and wounded, including eighteen terribly ill typhus patients. Today most people are vaccinated against this bacterial disease that is spread by lice. It is easily prevented by routine good hygiene, and can usually be cured with antibiotics. But we didn't have either, so death from typhus was very common. Eventually, I also contracted the disease. In a way, however, even though I was burning up with fever, I was lucky. This is because we ended up staying in one place for a whole month. So at least I didn't have to be on the run while I was sick. The reason for this monthlong stop, however, wasn't so lucky. It was because we had accumulated an awful lot of wounded and sick people, and we were also lacking in ammunition, dynamite, and medications.

This camp was near a huge and very deep lake, which was solidly frozen. So the partisans decided to make an airfield out of it. Right there on the ice! And so we did. Airplanes from Russia came in at night—landing on ice—with their lights and noisy engines turned off! They glided in through the darkness, bringing ammunition and medications, blankets, and clothing. They also evacuated the sick and wounded. Everything had to happen fast, so they could get back in the air before being spotted. The partisans scurried around as quietly as possible, unloading the supplies . . . everyone was silently slipping and falling. Each night when they left, the Russians took some of the sick and wounded with them. Can you imagine all this activity going on at night in the winter, in the middle of a forest for a whole month?

In the midst of this, I was trying to help, but I got so sick that I couldn't even move. My brain was hazy and everything hurt. At some point, a woman doctor came to me and said, "My dear, you have to get out of the cold. Go and lay down, you're too sick to help here." I had been burning up with a high fever for about ten days. So I went to the so-called infirmary. When the fever finally broke, they transferred me to a safe house to recuperate. It was completely empty. I lay there alone for a couple of days. Then, two soldiers with rifles came to me and said, "Manya, you came to the partisans to work not to be sick." I told them that I hadn't chosen to be sick, but that didn't matter to them. It turned out that they needed me to go help another woman who had also come down with the fever. She was the mistress of a partisan leader and had been sent to another safe house to recover.* This turned out to be very fortunate for me. The woman and her lover were very kind to me, even though I was still too weak to really take care of her.

We were provided with a horse and wagon and a wonderful young man to be our driver. When he saw my condition, he said, "You sit—I'll do everything." And he did. During the five days we stayed there, he brought us food, and since the sick woman couldn't eat, I ate her food, too. Finally, for the first time that I could remember, I wasn't hungry.

Then, on the fifth night, the driver rushed to us shouting, "The Germans are surrounding us—we have to run." He urged me, "Come on, quickly— dress the sick woman." But for some reason, I couldn't move, and said, "I can't." No matter how hard I tried, I couldn't move my legs. I was in terrible pain. It was hard for me to hear. And I was terribly cold. So he dressed the other woman, put her on the buggy, and then he ran to tell the others that I wasn't moving. When they came to get me, I told them, "I'm not going anywhere." The battalion leader and the others tried to convince me, saying,

---

*NOTE: *Since no one knew if they would live another day, it was common for unmarried people to become couples, and live as much as possible as if they were married, in order to experience whatever comfort and love that was still possible. Women in these relationships were safer than women who were alone.*

"You know what's going to happen to you if you stay? The Germans will find you and they'll torture and kill you." At that point, my brain wasn't working anymore, and I just said, "Okay." But I couldn't move. So they left. And I stayed. I was left alone in that house.

It turned out that in that area there was a sympathetic Gentile girl from my hometown who had seen me. So she knew that one partisan girl was left alone. The fact that I'd refused to go, she didn't know, so she thought I'd been abandoned. And she decided to help me. So she sent me a young man with a horse and buggy. And he came and called to me, "Come on, we're going to catch up with the partisans. They couldn't have gotten too far." He also had another girl with him. So he took me in the buggy, and when he noticed that I was shivering, he asked if I was cold. And I said, "Oh yes, I am terribly cold." He said, "Okay, I'll tell you what, I'm going to let you off at a farmer's house, and you can stay there and get warm, and tomorrow I'll come and get you."

So he knocked on the door and he said to the farmer, "Listen, I have a girl here, she's not well. Could we leave her here for a while? But I warn you, she's a partisan so don't do anything bad to her. I'll be back to get her in a day or so." Well, a day went by, two days went by, and nobody's there. I found out later that after he left the village, he had driven only about five kilometers, when the Germans caught up with him, and killed him and the girl. So this was yet another time because of a kind Polish Gentile, I was lucky.

With the Germans getting so close, the farmer was afraid to keep me any longer. He knew there were some Jews, who weren't partisans, hiding in a nearby village. So he went to them and he said, "Listen, I have one of your own. Why don't you come and get her?" And despite the danger, these brave Jews, who didn't know me, came to the farmer's house, but they didn't come in. They spoke to me through the window, and they saw that I was very sick. I was able to tell them that my father, sister, brother, and I belonged to the Kovpaks. So they made a deal with the farmer: if he would keep me a little longer, they would bring him meat, which was almost impossible to find. So he agreed, and the next day they brought him some meat. My good fortune did not last long, however. The following day, the farmer's little boy came running into the house, screaming, "Papa, the Germans are in the village!"

So the farmer said, "We have to get her out of here." He told the little boy to take me to the house where the Jews were. They took me in, but that night, when the Germans came into the village, they had to run to the forest. They asked if I wanted to come along, but I still was too sick to run. So again I said, "No, I'm not going. I'm cold and I'm not going anywhere." And they left. That night, the whole population of the village, not just the Jews, had run away into the forest. They knew that the Germans would kill them for helping partisans, even though for some of them, they really hadn't had a choice. They'd had to comply with the partisans' orders. But their motivations weren't as important as what they did. Again, I didn't feel so lucky . . . *but again, I was.*

So there I was, left by myself in a house. In one room there was what we called a "Russian" oven. On one side, you could have a fire for cooking, and on the other side there was an opening, like a ledge, where you could sleep. So I went on the oven ledge and I slept. That night a group of partisans were passing by the village. When they saw that all the homes were empty, they decided to find a place to sleep. They came to the house I was in. They brought in hay and put it on the floor to sleep on. Then, much to their surprise, they saw a person was sleeping on the oven ledge. Me. We talked for a while and I told them I was with the Kovpaks. It felt good to be able to talk with friends. I soon fell asleep, and when I woke up the next morning they were gone.

That afternoon, I saw tanks coming in, tanks with German soldiers, who must have been on the partisans' trail. I knew I had to hide fast. So I took the ladder and pulled it to the wall inside the house, and I went up into the attic. And through a crack in the wall I could see Germans right across the street. They were wrecking a house that had once been a local partisan headquarters. They began shooting their machine guns outside and inside, at the walls, at the furniture, and especially at the posters of Lenin and Stalin that had been left behind. Terrifying as it was, all of a sudden I had gotten very cold. I must have gone into shock, because I wasn't thinking clearly. I thought, "I don't give a damn, I'm going down." I took the ladder, went down, got back on the oven ledge, and went to sleep. At that point, death no longer meant anything to me.

Later, a group of Germans came into the house and saw me. They pointed their rifles at me and asked me who I was. Even in my confused state of mind, somehow I knew I should not let them know that I understood German. So I acted a little crazy, and pretended that I didn't know what they were saying. I repeated in Polish, "I am Polish. I am Polish. And I'm sick." After that, I said nothing. They communicated to me that they would be staying in the house overnight and that I should make them dinner. They brought out a lot of food: bread, salami, eggs, cheeses, tea. And I made scrambled eggs for them. When they sat down to eat, they indicated that I should join them at the table. So I joined them. I sat at a dinner table with Germans! And they shared everything they had with me. And I ate. And ate. And in their conversation they asked each other, "Who do you think she is? What nationality is she really? Do you think she's crazy?" Since I did understand German, I knew everything that they were saying, but I didn't bat an eye. I just kept wondering when they were going to kill me.

After they finished dinner, I cleaned up and went back to the oven ledge. The Germans made a lot of noise—constantly shooting—all night because they were afraid partisans were nearby and would attack them. They wanted the partisans to think that there were a lot of them and that they were heavily armed. They also wanted to distract the partisans because some small German airplanes were coming to pick up the bodies of Germans who had been killed by partisan land mines. Even with all that noise, I still fell asleep.

When I woke up, there was a complete quiet. And I realized that there were no Germans in the house. Peeking out the window, I saw that it had snowed heavily during the night. I walked outside, and there were no Germans on the street. Nobody was there. Empty. Everything covered in snow. Like a frozen ghost town. And just then, after two weeks of being in a kind of crazy, hazy, blackout, my head suddenly cleared from my sickness, and I wasn't freezing. Just like that. I was able to think clearly enough to start making an escape plan for myself. I still can't explain it. I wandered into another vacant house and found a toothbrush, a piece of bread, some salt and matches, all of which I put in my pockets. I knew that I'd be able to use them. And then I just walked around. There were cats and dogs and chickens and cows roaming through the snowy streets, but no people.

I went back to the house where I'd been staying, and just sat in a chair, staring off into space. Soon, little-by-little, the villagers started coming back to their homes. Apparently, the Germans, for whom I'd cooked, had been a non-Nazi infantry group of the *Wehrmacht,* the regular army, which is probably why they didn't kill me. When they'd left the village, they soon encountered the terrified villagers, hiding in the forest. The Germans assured them that they weren't in danger, and that it was safe for them to return to their homes. And, of course, when they did return to their homes, there I was, sitting in one of them. I must have looked like a lunatic, because when the lady of the house walked through the door and saw me, she almost had a heart attack. She crossed herself and cried out, "You! You're the crazy Jewess! What are you doing here?" To her, it looked like some kind of miracle, so she ran to her neighbors to tell them—and they all came rushing to look at me. It was like an inspection. They were saying, "Look at her! The Germans didn't kill the Jewess! What's going on?" The fact that the Germans left me alone and alive was such a miracle that the woman decided to let me stay.

That night, we worked hard baking potatoes and boiling a huge pot of cabbage soup. The room had gotten very hot, and suddenly it felt like the steam was actually coming right out of my head. I felt weak and confused, but at the same time, knew that I was in danger. I really needed to get out and rejoin the partisans. I would have left right then, but I had a splitting headache, so I lay down for a while. At about four o'clock in the morning, we were startled awake by a terrible noise outside. We took a look through the window and saw that the village was full of German tanks with German soldiers and all kinds of weapons. I knew I had to move fast, so I asked her if we could trade clothes so I would look like a farm girl. But she refused, and threatened to turn me over to the Germans. Then there was loud pounding on the door. I hid and held my breath. It was a German demanding food for his horse. The woman gave food to him, and when she followed him outside into the still-dark street, I figured that she was telling him about the crazy Jewess inside her house. So I just walked out of the door, hoping that in the blinding snowstorm, they wouldn't see me. The forest was about 500 meters away, and I calmly walked toward the forest. I just kept on walking all alone in the dark, on that snowy road. Suddenly, I heard yelling, and saw some farmers rushing toward me in their horse and buggy, waving and shouting, "What's going on in the village?" I replied, "I don't know, some Germans came in." And then I turned around and saw that the whole village was on fire. The Germans had come and burned it all down. Was I lucky again?

I kept walking. I was terribly cold and terribly hungry. I eventually saw several small farmhouses that were situated around a piece of farmland. I went to the door of one house and saw several farmers sitting around the table eating pancakes. My stomach was growling. Apparently, they had heard about me because when they saw me, they shouted, "Oh, look who is here, it's the crazy Jewess. They asked me what I wanted. I answered, "Could you give me something to eat?" They said, "Get out of here, you dirty Jew. It's because of you that all of these terrible things are happening." Somehow, instead of being intimidated, and running from them, I stood my ground and shouted back, "Okay, so you think you'll escape it? You'll have the same end like we had." And I turned and left. Later on I learned that about a half an hour after I'd left, the Germans came and killed those farmers right at that table. So it was lucky for me that they'd turned me away.

I kept on walking until I saw a house on fire, and I thought maybe at least I could get warm if I stood near it. As I got closer, I saw a German standing near the house, also getting warm. At that point, I thought, "I have to get warm. I really don't care anymore. I don't care if he kills me." So, convinced that I was going to get shot, I started walking towards the house. And as I approached it, I couldn't believe what I was seeing. The German left. He just walked away. More good luck. So I got warm, slept a bit on the ground, and then started walking again.

When I came to another farmhouse and knocked on the door, the man who answered was friendly. He said, "Listen, my dear. I know who you are. Don't worry. Come in. We're all in the same shoes. The Germans were killing the Jews, now they're killing the Gentiles. So come in the house and we'll feed you." And then he asked, "Do you know that the Jews that had been hiding in Berezhki in that village, are now hiding not far from here? After you eat, my two boys will take you to them." I was so relieved to know that even if I didn't get to live, at least I would get to die with my own people.

Later, when I set off with the boys, the snow came up past our waists, my legs hurt, and I was feeling sick again. But I walked and walked with the boys until we came to an open area in that forest. They told me that if I crossed the open area, that I'd find my Jewish people, they wished me well and left. By the time I got across the field to the Jewish camp, however, the Jews had left. Instead, there was a group of around ten Gentile farm families who seemed to be very well-organized and well-supplied. They had horses and buggies. They had sheepskin coats. They had hay. They had pillows. And food! They had dried food, but nevertheless, food. I decided to risk telling them that I was Jewish, and was relieved when they said, "Okay, listen, don't worry about it. You come. And whatever will happen to us, will happen to you." So I said,

"Okay," and was very grateful when they gave me something to eat. They thought they were safe because they knew the area well, and that the Germans would never follow them into the thick forest. They also had scouts out in all four directions, watching whichever way the Germans were going.

It looked like a good set-up, so I decided to stay with them. That night I went to sleep on the ground next to the horses, but I was freezing. When I woke up, I had so much snow on me that my feet had frozen completely. I couldn't stand up on my legs. And then, out of the blue, while I was trying to get up, the farmers just started beating me up. Apparently, for some reason, during the night they had decided that I was a spy. They cursed me, accusing me of being a spy, screaming that it was because of the Jews that the war had started. They screamed at me to get out of their camp. What could I do? I couldn't even stand up. So I yelled back, "You know what? If you want to kill me, go ahead—I'm in your hands. But I'm not leaving. I'm staying here with you." Why they stopped beating me, and let me stay, I'll never know.

For the next ten days, we stayed there. The whole time with no fire, because the smoke could be seen from a distance. I dragged myself to a little makeshift hut just big enough for me to lie down in, and stayed there by myself, sneaking out at night to steal food from them. When I woke up one morning, it was as if they had vanished. The farmers had left with the Russians. So then I was by myself. And now there was no one to steal food from. So I snuck around the empty camp and found an old piece of bread. Then, I crawled a little bit into the forest and found some berries. Eventually, I crawled all the way into the empty village and looked in the wells and cellars of burned-out houses. I miraculously found a pot, and two dead chickens. Much as I wanted to stay in one of the houses, I knew I wasn't safe there, so I struggled back to my hut. When I got there, I made a little fire, and using snow for water, I boiled the chicken. Just like that. Alone in the middle of nowhere. Nineteen years old, sick and unable to walk. I made delicious chicken soup. And finally, with a full stomach for the first time in many months, and thinking that maybe the worst was over, I went to sleep.

After a few days, a small group of partisans came by and invited me to join them. We made a camp further in the forest, and found some dirty old hay to sleep on. Very soon we all started itching like crazy—here—there—everywhere we were itching—nowhere on our bodies was safe. We thought we had chicken pox and scratched until we were bleeding. Still, we'd get up in the morning and sing and eat potatoes, figuring that the chicken pox would eventually go away. But they didn't. They got worse. One day, a doctor from a passing group of partisans noticed us and came over. We quickly showed him our "chicken pox." He told us that what we really had was *scabies*, and that the itchy rashes were caused by tiny mites that had burrowed into our skin. He told us to make a paste from the grease on a wagon's axle, and get fat from the inside of a pig. Then we should take off all of our clothes, and rub our entire bodies with the paste. We should scrub our clothes and then hold them up to the fire to burn off any remaining bugs. He also suggested that we look through our beds to see if there were any rats that might be carrying diseases. So we looked under the hay and sure enough, saw many, many huge, filthy, bug-infested rats staring right back at us. We found another place to sleep, and thankfully, the grease did help. We started healing, but it took a couple of weeks, and we ended up covered with scabs and scars.

We were alone in the middle of nowhere. After much discussion, we decided that since there were no longer any Germans nearby, that it would probably be safe to come out of hiding. But what did that actually mean? Where would we go? What would we do? How would we live? How would we be treated by the Gentiles? I decided to set off on my own to find some Gentiles who, instead of killing me, would maybe hire me to work around their homes and farms. And that's exactly what happened. I found a family to live with, and did whatever work needed to be done. The villagers tolerated me, the days turned into weeks, and life seemed pretty routine. Since we were very isolated, however, and had no idea about what was going on in the world outside the village, we never really felt safe.

One day, literally from out of nowhere, along came two girl partisans who had just been parachuted down by the Soviets. They wore uniforms, gun belts, and ammunition, and were dragging pallets of weapons, dynamite, ammunition, and medication to a group that was in the forest. This was a big deal for us, because the girls also had radios, and knew what was going on in the rest of the world. We were shocked and excited to learn that the Germans were finally being beaten! I told the girls that I'd been with the Kovpaks, so they invited me to join them. They gave me a rifle to carry, a radio to put on my shoulder, and bullets to wrap around my waist. It took two days and two nights for us to transport the supplies almost eighty kilometers through thick forests and miserable swamps. When we arrived, they invited me to stay with them, but I'd learned about a group of Jews that weren't too far away, and since I preferred to be with my own people, I thanked the Soviet partisans, told them goodbye, and set off to find the Jews.

I eventually found them, not far from the Pinsk area, where most of them had originally lived. They had escaped from a nearby German labor camp, and knew the area well. There were quite a few women, some teenagers, some small children, and old men. They had ten rifles—only one of which worked—the rest they used for spare parts. So with this one rifle, they would go out and secure themselves some food. They would go up to a farmer, act tough, and wave the rifle at him, so he felt that he had no choice but to give them food. Sometimes this would cause problems with anti-Semitic Soviets and Ukrainians who were also living in the forest, and who didn't want us competing with them for food. They would tell the farmers not to be afraid of us because Jews didn't know how to fight, and our weapons didn't work. So we ended up with reputations for being weak.

But our "weak" Jewish boys came up with a clever plan. They cut down a tree, chopped it into smaller pieces, and made a long triangle out of it. Then they carried it on their shoulders for about ten kilometers until they came to the train tracks. They attached the wooden triangle to the tracks and ran away. The next day, when a train came by, it was thrown completely off the tracks. There was a terrible commotion and a huge, smoking pile up! So now all of a sudden the Jews got a good reputation. They had strategies. They were tough. They were fearless fighters. They knew what to do. So then the farmers didn't hesitate to give us whatever we wanted: food, ammunition, guns, and even some dynamite. Anything that would get us to leave quickly.

Soon, our group decided to blow up a train whose tracks were only two kilometers away. So the boys organized a group of about fifteen or twenty, and they took me along as a nurse, in case someone got hurt. We even had a local guide who had grown up in the area. He knew one way to get us to that railway, and another way to come back. So on a very damp, foggy night, we approached the tracks, with each of us carrying a stick of "dynamite." It was like a piece of soap with a wick attached to it. The boys were going to insert the dynamite at intervals along a couple miles of the tracks. Then they would light the wicks—and run like crazy. The guide and I would stay back a bit in the trees, and wait for the boys to rejoin us after lighting the wicks. What a surprise we were in for when we got there. Apparently the Germans had chosen that very night to do some repair work on the tracks. Instead of being devoid of human beings, there was a crowd of workers. They'd lit several bonfires for light and warmth, and they even had built themselves a small temporary barracks nearby, so they could sleep in shifts. We were afraid we'd have to give up our plans.

But our boys refused to give up, and decided to sneak out to darker spots of the tracks that weren't currently being worked on. Then, as planned, they'd position the dynamite, light it, and run. Before they could do this, however, they realized that they were in trouble. Their matches had gotten wet, and wouldn't ignite. So the boys started darting in and grabbing burning-hot coals from the Germans' bonfires to use to light the wicks. Of course, the Germans soon realized that something was going on, and started shooting. Our guide, who was not a partisan, said to me, "Oh no! I'm not staying here. I don't want to get killed! I'm running." Responding like a trained partisan, I said, "But we have our orders. We have to stay here. This is our gathering point." He said, "No, uh-uh," and took off. And then, unlike a trained partisan, I ran after him. This turned out to be lucky for me, because as soon as I started running, I saw that a German was already chasing me, screaming for me to "Halt!" I also heard, and felt, bullets zooming by as he got closer. I came to a big ditch and figured that I was done for. But I managed to leap across the ditch, and kept on running. Taking a quick look back, I saw that when the German had come to the ditch, for some reason, he just stopped. Again, I was lucky. Later, when everyone had returned to the camp, we were devastated to find out that one of our group had been killed. But we were also overjoyed that the dynamite had worked, and that the tracks had been terribly damaged. There would be no more laughing at the Jews. Our reputations as warriors were confirmed. It wasn't very long thereafter that the Germans were beaten back by the Soviets, and in July 1944, we were liberated in Pinsk.

Liberation was very exciting! We marched into Pinsk as proud partisans. Everyone cheered us for being heroes! We were jubilant that we had helped the Soviet Army win the war! The cheering soon died down, however, and was replaced by an insecurity that made everyone nervous. This was because many of the Pinsk Gentile residents had helped the Germans, and they were afraid of reprisals from both the Soviets and the Jews. I felt a little safer because I had found a job with the Soviet security police (NKVD). They paid us, but not much, and there wasn't anything to buy in Pinsk, there was never enough food, and I was always hungry, but I was able to rent a small room to live in. What I really needed, however, were shoes and clothing. And most especially, a warm coat. I was desperate for a coat.

At that time, there weren't any stores, but there was a huge warehouse full of used clothing and household goods. We were allowed into the warehouse to pick out whatever we needed. I was stunned when I noticed that each coat I picked up had a yellow Star of David sewn on it. In fact, all of the clothing in that warehouse had once belonged to Jews who had been sent to extermination camps. I can't explain the eerie, sickening sensation that enveloped me. I felt that I was walking through ghosts. And I felt guilty that I was now benefitting from the tragedy of my own people. Having no choice, however, I grabbed a coat, put it on, and walked away as fast as I could.

I worked at the NKVD for around a year. The working conditions there were terrible. Our office was in an ancient, unheated, and airless, cement monastery. Sometimes I had to work until one o'clock in the morning. One late night, when the temperature went below zero and I was starving, I thought, "This is not for me. I did not go through the Nazi years to end up dying here on my job." But leaving a job with the Soviets was not easy. Anyone who had a job felt lucky at first, but they soon learned that we were under total Soviet control. We couldn't just leave a job if we wanted to. For once, my bad eyes brought me good luck. I was able to get a letter from a doctor saying that I could not be out at night. So I was able to leave that terrible office. But then, of course, I no longer had a job.

I decided to go "home" to Dombrovitsa. I had the crazy idea that I wanted to see my house. I walked the whole way, almost sixty miles. And with each step, I felt that I was stepping on blood. When I finally got there, I was surprised to see that my house was still standing, and that it was empty. It hadn't been taken over by Poles. But I didn't have a penny to my name. I didn't have any food, I didn't have anything, so even with a house, I had no way to live. I saw some Gentiles in the village who had known me all my life. I thought maybe they'd be able to help me. But instead of being happy that I was alive, and greeting me warmly, they were angry and demanded to know how come I'd survived. They treated me as if I didn't deserve to live.

I soon learned the terrible fate of my fellow Kovpaks: They had been involved in a horrific attack in which over half of them had been killed, including my beloved father and sister. They died fighting. They were heroes. To this day, I remember each and every one of them, how courageous they were, and I say *Kaddish* (the Jewish prayer for the dead) for them.

So even though I had a house, I knew I couldn't live in it. I couldn't live in that village with those hate-filled people, with those painful memories. I knew that I would have to sell the house. But who could buy a house then? Who would buy a house from a Jew? But then I was approached by a Gentile man who had figured out how to do it. He sold a pig and gave me the money. And that's the only money I got for my house. Then I ran away from my home town. And I vowed that I would never set foot there again. And I never did.

By January 1947, it was clear that I had to get out of Poland, but I had nowhere to go, and no way to get there. With so many Jews wandering around in the same situation, however, I learned from a group of new friends about the displaced persons' camps that the Allies had set up in Berlin. At that point, there were thirty of us, and we just decided to go. Why not? There were many black-marketeers who were renting out trucks and drivers to take Jews out of Poland. It was a big business. For an additional price, they also took care of bribing the border guards so they wouldn't search the trucks, or demand to see our papers—which we didn't have. We were soon able to get a truck and driver, and began our long journey. When we finally got to the border, we each held our breath while the driver took care of the necessary bribes. And before we knew it, we had crossed out of Poland! It was strange that suddenly, we could be free in Germany . . . the very country that had almost succeeded in removing us all from the face of the earth.

A few miles later, our happiness came to an abrupt end when the truck broke down in the snow. So there we were. Stranded. Illegal. In the middle of nowhere. And as usual, I was freezing. So I'm sitting there and I'm shivering. And all of a sudden two of the men say, "That's it. Who wants to walk—to walk to Berlin?" And without any thought at all, I jumped up and said, "I do." And we started walking. And we walked. And walked. Finally, we came to the train station in a very small town. As we arrived, we noticed that the townspeople were watching us nervously, and staying as far away from us as possible. We were raggedy, and strange-looking to them, so they were afraid of us. And naturally, since we looked so different from everyone else, the police arrested us right away and took us to the police station. And also right away, they started questioning us. They wanted to know who we were, how we got there, where we were going, and most importantly, how soon we

Manya Barman
Berlin, Germany,
1947

would leave. We couldn't say that we came in a truck with a bunch of stateless Jewish refugees, and that they were stranded out there somewhere. We did have to tell them that we were Jews, however, because my two companions had been in concentration camps and had identification numbers tattooed on their arms.[27] So we said that we had just come across the border on foot. And that our goal was to get to a displaced persons' camp in Berlin. Following that, we would go as soon as possible to Palestine. The police were very rude and rough with us. They said they were going to send us back to Poland. But we argued, telling them, "You might as well just kill us now, because we are not going back to Poland." Finally, they gave in, and put us on the train to Berlin. So we took a train, which was illegal since we were refugees and didn't have any citizenship documents. Fortunately, no one asked us for our papers.

---

27. In order to keep accurate records, the Germans tattooed Auschwitz inmates with numbers on their left forearm.

The first thing we did when we finally got to Berlin was to contact the black market owner of the truck that had broken down. Fortunately, he was an honest man, and quickly sent another truck to get the rest of our group. Then we found a small displaced persons' camp in the French Sector that would take us in. Since only two hundred Jews lived there, we got to know each other quickly. The camp was very well-organized. We were given food, and a place to wash up and sleep. And, just like in Pinsk, there was a huge warehouse, which I knew would be filled with piles of clothes . . . clothes from extermination camps . . . the clothing of dead Jewish men, women, and children. A skirt that could have originally belonged to a relative . . . a sweater that might have been a friend's. This time, since my own clothes were nothing more than filthy rags, I had no choice but to take what I needed. And as I put each piece on, I said *Kaddish* for the woman who'd worn it before me.

Our days in the camp were filled with a sense of the urgency of life itself. We had to get on fast with being alive—who knew how long it would last? There were seemingly endless activities, including secular and Jewish schools as well as recreation for the children and adults. There were newspapers, a library, a choir, a theater group, a synagogue. And strange as it might sound, we refugees—we homeless, displaced people—inside this camp, we were better off than the "free" Germans who were outside. The same Germans who had wanted to exterminate us. They came knocking on the gate at night, carrying their sick and weakened children, begging, crying that they were starving . . . and they were. They were hungry, cold, weak, sick, and hopeless. Their city and their homes were completely bombed out. They had nothing. Some of us gave them food.

Within the camp, our lives went on with a semblance of normalcy. Because there were so many of us who were young adults, many became couples and quickly got married. In fact, that's where I met the wonderful man who would become my husband, Herman Auster. He already had a black market business that was going well, and had come to the camp to meet a contact person who had just arrived at that camp from Poland. We fell in love. And in 1948, we got married in that displaced persons' camp. We soon were able to move into an apartment he'd found for us in Berlin, and in 1949, our first son, Barry, was born there. We had become part of a community of young Jewish families who were planning to stay temporarily in Berlin until we could go to Palestine. Much to our frustration, however, the temporary situation stretched out longer and longer, because the British wouldn't let us into Palestine.[28] Even after 1948, when Israel had become an independent country, living conditions there were not so good, and now that we were parents, the idea of living as farmers on a *kibbutz* (a collective farm), was not very appealing.

In 1950, the United States suddenly passed a law easing up their strict immigration process for European war refugees.* Since my husband, who knew the Russians well, was nervous about the growing power of the Soviets in East Berlin and East Germany, we knew that it was time to get out. Once our decision was made, we wasted no time in moving to Detroit, where we had friends who were also survivors. They were doing well in the meat business, and my husband joined them. I went to Midrasha Hebrew College for five years and became certified as a Hebrew teacher. In 1952, we were blessed with the birth of our second son, Steven. My husband worked hard and made a very nice life for us. Along with other young Survivor parents, we brought up our families and lived good lives in America. We were friendly with Gentiles, but since our experiences were so different, we felt most comfortable with other Holocaust survivors. We never had to explain anything about our past. Many times, we didn't even have to talk. Sitting together in silence said more than words.

As time passed, we lived a good life and counted our blessings. My husband even bought some farmland so we would be property owners, and if necessary, we'd always be able to feed ourselves. We actually tried to farm it, but soon realized that we were city people, so we sold all but forty acres, and returned to the city, where we knew how to make a decent living. Unfortunately, our good luck would not last. Within a few months, it became clear that my beloved husband was very ill. He was only fifty-nine when we lost him, and we were devastated. He had been a wonderful husband and father. Everyone who knew him, loved him. My years with him had been the only

---

Ironically, this action also allowed Nazi war criminals to evade capture and punishment by pretending to be refugees coming to America.

28. At the end of World War II, Palestine was still under British administration (the British Mandate). The British government wanted to placate Arab countries, so it continued its strict pre-war restrictions on Jewish immigration to Palestine. The prohibition against the immigration of Jewish refugees to Israel was known as *The British Blockade.*

time since my early childhood that I had felt safe, cared for, and hopeful about the future. I felt totally lost. Yes, I'd been lost before, but then I'd been on my own. This time, I was the mother of two sons. So I couldn't stay lost for long. I began teaching at a Hebrew School, and when it was financially necessary, I would sell a few acres of the farmland that my husband had left us.

Years passed, and I married a second time, to Henry Feldman, but years later, when I was again widowed, I decided to remain on my own. Through the years, I have stayed active in the Jewish community, as a member of organizations, and as a volunteer. Until recently, I have also spoken to schools and community groups about the Holocaust on a regular basis. I was also involved with the founding of the Detroit Holocaust Memorial Center, and often spoke to groups there. I am deeply honored to be featured in the "Portraits of Honor: Our Michigan Holocaust Survivors" exhibit[29] at the Holocaust Memorial Center Zekelman Family Campus, in Farmington Hills, Michigan.

Well, it's already 2014 and I'm ninety-one years old. How did the time go so fast? As I look back, I see that my life has been full of surprises . . . and they weren't all bad. Each time I thought it was the end, something else happened. I had some good luck, and found another way to stay alive. I was committed to living a good, loving, Jewish life—to treasure the life I was given, when so many others didn't get the chance. Even now, in my nineties, with my health not so good, and it's hard to get around—or even see or hear—you might think that nothing new would happen. But you'd be surprised. Yes, there are still surprises. Would you believe that last year I was asked to be part of a theatrical performance and documentary film? It was part of a project put on by the Detroit Witness Theater. Over several months, they brought together Holocaust survivors and students to discuss and record their life stories. Transcripts from our conversations provided the basis for a script. Then we rehearsed and put together a theatrical performance in April 2012, at the Jewish Community Center's Berman Center for the Performing

---

29. For more information about Manya and the other Holocaust survivors featured in this extraordinary exhibit, please see the Holocaust Memorial Center website: www.portraitsofhonor.org. Another outstanding website that includes an interview with Manya is that of the *Voice/Vision Holocaust Survivor Oral History Archive* at http://holocaust.umd.umich.edu/began.

Detroit Witness Theater cast members,
Phillip McMurray, Manya Feldman and
Erica Schman, West Bloomfield, Michigan, 2013

Arts in West Bloomfield, Michigan. The title of the production is, "We Are Here: The Journey from Harmony to Horror to Hope." [30] It was such a joy to work with these young people—we laughed and cried together, and became like a family. They gave me hope for the future. I think I learned as much from them as they learned from me.

Despite the numerous losses and the sadness, in many ways, I know that I have been lucky. I was lucky each time I survived an attack or an illness. I was

---

30. "We Are Here" is a well-known Yiddish phrase, *mir zaynen doh*, dating from ancient times. It was a symbol both of Jewish Zionist presence in Palestine and of Jewish resistance to the Nazis. The phrase is immortalized in what is known as the partisans' anthem, "*Zog Nit Keyn Mol,*" written by Hirsh Glick in 1943, and now sung at Jewish memorial services all over the world.

lucky to find love. Lucky to find joy. Lucky to have two wonderful, accomplished sons—both doctors—beautiful, intelligent daughters-in-law, and four bright, talented, loving granddaughters. I am especially blessed to now have an extraordinary great-granddaughter—a fourth generation! Because of them, I feel that my life has been worthwhile. That I have accomplished something. I hope to be remembered as an honorable woman who, despite the horror, was lucky, and stayed strong. A woman who loved and was committed to her family, to the Jewish people, and who did everything she could to make sure that those who died in the Holocaust would not be forgotten. I hope I have inspired others to fight oppression.

Before you go, here's one more memory I'd like to share with you. One time when my son, Barry, was already out of high school, he said, "Mom, I never wanted to tell you, but now, I will. One day I was walking in a hall in high school, and a guy came up to me and grabbed me, and threw me up against the wall, and said, 'You dirty Jew, I hate your guts.'" Shocked, I asked my son, "So why didn't you tell me?" and he told me, "Mom, you would have raised hell." And you know what? I would have.

Manya Feldman stands in front of her section of
the "Portraits of Honor" Exhibit,
Holocaust Memorial Center Zekelman Family Campus,
Farmington Hills, Michigan, 2012

*"Many people say that the Jews went silently . . . like sheep
to the slaughter. This is absolutely not true.
I was there. I saw it. I lived it.
I photographed it."*

Chapter 4

Faye Lazebnik Schulman

1924, Lenin, Poland—Toronto, Ontario, Canada

Faye Lazebnik
Lenin, Poland 1941

Faye Schulman
Toronto, Ontario 2013

I n the bright light that streamed from her modern apartment when she opened the door to greet me, tiny Faye Schulman looked as if she were floating on a sunbeam. Her eyes sparkled with their own secret energy, as she smiled and welcomed me into her lovely, art-filled home. Her eyes also conveyed a sense of her profound knowledge of the human soul. At 90 years of age, this tiny, beautiful woman still radiates the calm confidence that must have provided comfort and inspiration to her patients as well as to the partisans who fought at her side against the Germans in the Polesi forest during World War II.

With the Toronto skyline as our backdrop, we sat companionably in Faye's living room. Once she was sure that I was comfortable, and had everything I needed, she began telling me her story, just as if we were old friends, who visited often, and were picking up where our last conversation had left off. And as she spoke, her tiny physique seemed to transform into the impressive stature of the strong, undaunted woman-warrior that she still is today. I could almost feel the heat when she told me about how, as a partisan, she set her beloved childhood home on fire so that the Germans couldn't use it for their headquarters. I silently cheered at the bittersweet moment when the Germans decided that her skills as a photographer made her "valuable" enough to be allowed to live—at least for a while. I could see her performing surgery out in the freezing cold Polish forest, while bullets flew over her head. I was awed by the movie star, glamorous young woman in a luxurious, leopard-fur coat and hat, confidently lifting her rifle to shoot an enemy that was determined to kill her.

Alternately gracious or fiery, authoritative or spunky—Faye Schulman's multifaceted personality still is as adaptable and engaging today, as it was seventy years ago—when she made a Nazi mass-murderer smile, and persuaded tough, Soviet partisans to take her along with them. What is also unchanged over seventy years, is her agonized grief over the tragic fate of so many loved ones . . . the lost Jews of Europe, and her determination to make sure the world never forgets.

Here is Faye's story . . .

Toronto, Ontario, Canada, 2012

I was born into a large, very close, religious Jewish family that included my parents, Yakov and Rayzel Lazebnik, and my six siblings. My oldest sister, Sonia, was married to Rabbi Yitzhak Koziolek, and they had two small children. My next sister, Esther, was married to a doctor, Meyer Feldman. My oldest brother, Moishe, was a photographer, and my next brother, Kopel, was a Yeshiva student. My two little brothers were Grainom and Boruch. We lived in Lenin, a town on the eastern edge of Poland. Many outsiders think that our village was named after Vladimir Ilyich Lenin, the man who led the Russian Revolution. But since our village, along with its Jewish population, goes all the way back to the early 1700s, it was in existence long before Mr. Lenin, so there isn't any connection between the two.

From the late 1700s until the end of World War I, our town found itself inside an unusual area known as the "Pale of Settlement," the artificially created territory where Imperial Russia had relocated its Jews. Lenin would probably have been just another typical Eastern European town, had it not been for its unique location on the River Sluch. Poland and Russia seemed to always be fighting over this region. We often said, "You could go to sleep one night in Poland and wake up the next morning in Russia, or the Soviet Union, without ever walking out of your front door." During my family's time there, Lenin had been under the control of Imperial Russia, then Poland, then the communist Soviet Union, and then, in 1941, Nazi Germany. Today, it is located in Belarus.

Sometimes our small river, with its little wooden footbridge, became the border separating us from Russia, thereby giving Lenin status as an international border town. Along with Lenin's changing borders, the status of its Jews could also change from one night to the next morning, depending on what government was in charge. For instance, in 1939, when Germany and Russia signed their so-called "non-aggression" pact, dividing Poland in half, the Soviet border just moved westward. Suddenly, we belonged to the USSR instead of Poland or Nazi Germany. So our beautiful little Lenin, whose Jewish and Gentile citizens only wanted to live in peace—and who did a pretty good job of it when left to themselves—was often embattled and occupied by foreigners. With no other choice, we got used to it, and didn't really care who was in charge—as long as they allowed us to live our lives.

Between the end of World War I in 1918, and the German invasion of Poland in 1939, we were under Polish control, so that was the way I'd known Lenin. And since we were then an international border town, we always had thousands of Polish military personnel everywhere. They had built an impressive modern building for their headquarters, and barracks to house the soldiers who were assigned to guard our town. All these guards were a great benefit to our economy. In fact, our economy depended on them. Whether they needed secretaries, bookkeepers, craftsmen, tailors, merchandise from stores, or even a good photographer, they always knew where to go. Our family was particularly happy to have them, because they frequented the little restaurant my mother had set up in our kitchen. The money this business brought in supported us. Another reason we were glad there were so many guards in town was that the crime rate was almost nonexistent. So we didn't have to worry about anti-Semitic Polish peasants coming to town to attack us.

Living at an international border, however, did present some disadvantages for both Jews and Gentiles. Security was very tight. People needed special visas to get in or out, and this created a hardship for families with relatives who lived out of town. Furthermore, there was a frustrating nighttime curfew for everyone. We all had to be off the streets by dark, which was difficult in the winter when darkness came so early. It was especially challenging for teenagers who wanted to socialize or carry on romances at night. We did manage to elude the authorities when necessary, and at that time it was even an adventure. I had no idea that this sneaking around would soon become a skill that would help to keep me alive.

As an international border town, Lenin provided a gateway for other Europeans who were going to the Soviet Union, and vice versa. Outsiders were constantly going back and forth, so despite being located in the middle of thick forests, swamps, and marshland, we weren't totally isolated from the outside world. And because of this, we were able to keep up on current world events. Of primary importance for the Jews, of course, was any news about Poland, the country that controlled us, and Palestine, the Jewish homeland, where we hoped to live one day. It was common for Jewish teenagers to belong to various Zionist groups that provided preparation for a future in our own country.

The Polish military wasn't alone in guarding the border. On the Soviet side, there was also a large contingent of soldiers making sure we didn't cross the little bridge to their huge country. The bridge had a border-gate at the center, complete with a guarded Polish booth on one side, and a guarded Soviet booth on the other. In addition, a fence had been built down the middle of the little river. It was particularly frustrating that the river was so closely controlled during the hot summer months, when we would have loved to go swimming. Maybe the Soviets were afraid that we'd swim across to their country. And whereas when we were children, swimming across to their country never entered our minds, a few years later—when the Germans came—crossing this water would often be on our minds.

So the Polish and Soviet guards made sure no one ventured to each other's side, and although during that time, there was as no actual fighting, sometimes the two sides did seem to be competing with each other in showing off their military power. Who had the better-looking uniforms? The shiniest boots? Who marched with more enthusiasm? Who displayed the most threatening looks on their faces? I often wondered if these guards, who were just young men, far away from home, weren't also chatting and telling each other jokes during their long, boring hours of guard duty.

My family lived in a beautiful, large home that had been lovingly designed and built by my father. We valued education, and studied hard. It was common for Jewish children to know five or six languages, and we learned these in the normal course of our days. Yiddish was spoken in our homes, so it was our first language. Then, from age five to age fourteen, we attended Polish school, where only Polish was spoken. Every day after Polish school, Jewish children went to Hebrew school. And when we were out in the streets, we spoke Belarus, also known as "White Russian." This is the language that was spoken by the local Gentile Lenin population, who were ethnic White Russians,[31] instead of Poles. So we were always thinking and speaking different languages—sometimes in the same sentence! Additionally, since we were neighbors with the Soviet Union, which had formerly been Russia, we also could speak some Russian. Of course, when the Soviets occupied Lenin in 1939, we picked up as much of their language as quickly as we could. Even

31. *White Russians*, also known as *Belarusians* (from the Slavic word, *bela*, for "white "), are Slavic people who live in what is now the country of Belarus.

though it was annoying at the time, I did learn to speak perfect Russian, which would help me later when I joined the Soviet partisans. Something else that would help me when I joined the partisans is that I was healthy, very strong, and already used to hard work. This is because Mama always made me do heavy chores, such as sending me to bring water from the community's well, and helping Papa chop the wood.

Just before World War II, since Lenin was a Polish town, it was subject to the recently imposed anti-Semitic laws of Poland. So Jews were now banned from attending universities, which made it impossible for them to become professionals. Jews also were prohibited from holding public office, so participating in, interacting with, or even influencing the government was always a problem. Aside from the government, however, since around half of Lenin's 12,000 people were Jews, there was no big majority/minority competition, and no one felt outnumbered. Furthermore, the Gentile Belarusians didn't share the anti-Semitic attitudes so common among the Poles. We had a sense that we should stick together, so we helped and depended on each other—we were happy for each other's good news, and shared each other's sorrow. Outside of town, however, with the largely anti-Semitic Polish peasants, it was a different story. And in 1941, when the Germans broke their Non-Aggression pact by invading the Soviet Union, being a Jew suddenly became a daily life and death challenge.

My father, who was very religious, was too generous to be successful in business, always giving credit and merchandise to customers who couldn't pay. Eventually, he ended his various businesses, and devoted most of his time to the synagogue and Jewish community, where he was held in high esteem. This left my mother to support us, which she did with small business ventures, like the restaurant in our kitchen. Even though we were poor, my parents made sure that my older brother, Moishe, who as a Jew wasn't allowed to pursue a university education, learned a marketable skill. They sent him away to a photography school in Pinsk for his training. When he came home, he taught the rest of us everything he'd learned, so we could help. As a very artistic child, I was particularly interested in photography, and was honored when he asked me to be his assistant. And because of the Polish soldiers, who wanted to send photos home to their families, we had a good business. We were proud and happy to be able to contribute financially to our struggling family.

When Moishe married and moved to a nearby town to set up a photography business there, I went along and helped run it. We did well, and of course, sent money home to our parents to make their lives less difficult. I worked very hard, and in addition to taking photos, I even handled the business side of our studio. I was so professional, that few people knew I was just a young teenager. Using my artistic ability, I learned how to tint black and white photos (we only had black and white film then) into beautiful color portraits. These became very popular and increased our business. So even though my brother sometimes treated me like a little sister, I knew he depended on me, appreciated me, and was proud of me. I think my experiences living outside of Lenin opened my eyes to the different ways of the world, and made me even more independent than I already was. This independence, creativity, and ability to take on responsibility would help me later when I joined the partisans.

From 1939 until 1941, under the terms of the German-Soviet Non-Aggression Pact, the communist Soviets occupied Lenin, and the Polish soldiers suddenly were gone. I went back to my parents' house. Because of the communists' purported belief in sharing the wealth, life quickly and drastically changed for the wealthier townspeople. The Soviets considered them to be "capitalists," who had gained their wealth by exploiting poor workers. Their businesses and belongings were confiscated, and many were put in prison—or even sent to Siberia. Since we were poor, we had nothing to lose. We felt bad for the people who were sent away, but ironically, it turned out that they were spared from the Germans. The Soviets allowed me to work as a photographer, and my earnings, while not grand, allowed us to live relatively well. I was particularly fortunate that the Soviets required everyone to have identity cards, so I was very busy taking photos! I was even able to buy a beautiful leopard fur coat and hat—at a very good price—from a shipment that the Soviets had brought with them from Russia. Little did I know that my skill as a photographer—and that coat—would ultimately save my life.

On June 21, 1941, when the Germans broke their Non-Aggression Pact by attacking the Soviets, our most recent occupiers scrambled to get out of Lenin. With no warning, we were left for two days without any government at all, and therefore, without any security. As a consequence, we were immediately subjected to looting and abuse by anti-Semitic peasants. Much to our surprise, relief, and pride, these attacks were stopped by quickly-organized groups of young Jews. Instead of hiding in their homes, they armed themselves with rocks and sticks, and conspicuously stood guard, and didn't hesitate to fight. The peasant attacks stopped, but they were frightening foreshadows of the horrors that would come along with the Germans on June 24—horrors that could not be repelled by teenagers with rocks and sticks. In addition to occupying Lenin, the Germans used it as a gateway for invading the Soviet Union. So now, instead of travelers going back and forth, we had huge numbers of infantry, tanks, and weapons. And as the Germans came through on their way to fight the Soviets, they were especially enthusiastic about beating up Jews, and taking Jewish belongings. Their favorite recreational activities involved humiliating, injuring, and sometimes killing Jews. And they didn't care about age or gender. Unaccustomed to being hated or treated like vermin, we were stunned by the Germans' savagery. One day, for example, they barged into our house and forced my sister and me to stand facing a wall, while they pointed their guns at us, screamed hate-filled anti-Jewish obscenities, and shouted that we were about to die. Lucky for us, our attackers were suddenly called away. Too shaken to speak, we silently went on with our day.

All the Jews had to work, and as the equivalent of slave-labor, we were constantly being verbally and physically abused. At first, my job was to clean the homes that were now inhabited by the Germans. These houses had once belonged to my neighbors and friends. It was strange to now be cleaning rooms that I had known under such different, happier circumstances. Cleaning houses, however, was better than other jobs because I was at least inside, and even able to steal a little food to take home to my family. Sometimes that would be the only food we had.

Soon the same anti-Jewish regulations that we'd heard had been imposed in Eastern Poland, were now imposed on us. We all had to sew yellow Jewish Stars on the fronts and backs of our clothing, making us targets for insult and abuse. Then Jewish children were no longer allowed to attend public school. Then we were prohibited from walking on the sidewalks. Soon, Jews had to surrender all their gold, silver, artwork, antiques, furs—all valuables, including horses, cows, and chickens. Of course, I had to give them my beautiful leopard-fur coat and hat. Next, a *Judenrat* was put in command to make sure that all German directives would be followed to the letter. Jewish hostages were taken to ensure compliance. The infrequent arrival of food was barely enough to keep people alive, so we were always hungry and many soon be-came malnourished. While my parents tried to maintain some semblance of normalcy, each day brought even more misery than the day before. In the midst of the horror, however, I was surprised by, and very grateful for, the kindness of one German officer, whom I never met. He sometimes would leave a little food for me at the well where I got water every day. He soon disappeared, and I later learned that he had been arrested for not following German orders.

One day, something very unusual—and therefore very terrifying—happened. A high-ranking German officer walked into our home. He was big, very tall, and very clean. He wore an impeccably tailored uniform and tall, shiny, black leather boots. Everything about him was in perfect order. When we felt his presence in our doorway, we all stopped in the middle of whatever we'd been doing—fully expecting to be shot. Well, it turned out that somehow he knew I was a photographer. So instead of shooting us, he ordered me to make him a passport photo, warning me that if it wasn't ready in exactly one hour, that I would be executed. Well, in addition to taking the photo, I would have to process the film, and make a print in that one hour. Since film didn't dry in such a short time, trying to accomplish this task was a nightmare. I waved the film around, fanned it, and blew on it. Miracu-lously, by the time he returned, the passport photo was ready. He sneered at me and told me that I was a "very lucky Jew." It was frightening that the Germans already knew everything about us. Who had told them I was a pho-tographer?

Thanks to my photography skills, however, I was soon "employed" (mean-ing that I worked, but didn't get paid) by the Germans to develop the photos they were shooting. It seemed that they wanted to keep visual proof of their atrocities. To them, these pictures of unspeakable horror were prized trophies, which they collected, and showed others with pride. My so-called "job" be-came even more important to me on May 10, 1942. This was the day when, using strong wooden posts and barbed wire, the Germans suddenly enclosed a two-block area in what had previously been the most run-down section of town. This became Lenin's Jewish ghetto. Along with almost two thousand Jews, we were forced to move out of our home and into this ghetto, leaving behind everything but what we could carry. There would have been even more of us, but early in the German-occupation, some of Lenin's Jews had managed to escape to the forest. Of those who had not run away, all healthy men between the ages of fourteen and fifty, had been shipped to forced-labor camps . . . or worse.

Today, it's all but impossible to imagine up to fifty people crammed into each small, old house. And if it hadn't actually been our reality, it would have been impossible for us to imagine it even then. Conditions worsened daily, and with no strong men around to protect us, it was particularly dangerous to be a female. We were never safe from the random desires of the Germans, and so we always tried to stay out of their sight. As the frigid winter came, the lack of blankets and firewood, or even wooden furniture to burn, made it impossible to stay warm. It was impossible to stay clean, and almost everyone got sick. So there we were: unprotected, dirty, starving, freezing, frail, sick, terrified, and working at hard labor beyond any human capacity. The only break in this misery was the occasional help from a few extremely brave Gentiles, who risked not only their own lives, but the lives of their families, in order to smuggle food into the ghetto. I will never forget the courage of these kind and brave Christians.

Once again, my photography skills soon provided another benefit to me and my family. As part of my work for the Germans, I had been given a special permit to leave the ghetto so I could make use of the professional darkroom equipment still at our house. I remember wondering how it was possible that our house had been neither vandalized nor occupied by Germans. It had remained empty, and the darkroom was intact. I think that the Germans probably assigned someone to make sure the house was left alone, just so I could use the darkroom for them.

While I was outside of the ghetto, I could have easily escaped, but the Germans knew that I would not, since they would then kill my family. It was for this reason that most of the remaining young people, who could have escaped, also had chosen instead to stay, suffer, and even die, with their families. Today, when I hear someone confidently insist that they never would have stuck around and put up with the Germans, I remind them that things are rarely as simple as they might seem now. When I explain that escaping would have brought brutality and death to their families, and that even random additional people could also be executed, just so the Germans could show what would happen if anyone escaped, they start to see things differently. The deaths of innocent people was too big a burden for most of us to take on. When I was outside of the ghetto, however, I was able to barter with farmers for some food to sneak back to my family. And I also managed to hide a few pieces of equipment, some chemicals, and film, in case I might need them later.

Early one morning, we were ordered to assemble just outside the ghetto gate for our first "roundup." Believing that we were about to be executed, we just stood there stunned, awaiting the inevitable. So we were shocked when the Germans merely counted us, checked our names, and sent us back to the ghetto. Then they found and killed anyone who hadn't been at the assembly. Not knowing what else to do, I kept busy at my photography, hid whatever equipment I could, and stayed alert for signs of impending danger . . . which unfortunately, didn't take long to appear.

One day, I was called to headquarters to take a photo for a special portrait of the top Nazi official. This "man" was a known mass-murderer. And that's just what he looked like. He had the eyes of a killer. As I was setting up my camera, he warned me that I would be executed if the picture wasn't "good." I had no idea how he defined "good." Did he want to look like the crazed mass-murderer that he was? Did he want to look like a normal human being? When I saw the result of the first photo, in which he was glaring at the camera, I was certain that he would kill me. Unsure of how to escape his wrath, I decided to take an additional picture, telling him that the first one was no good. And for the second one, I did the unthinkable. I just used my usual "photographer's voice," and told him to smile. I even surprised myself. Where did I—a small Jewish girl—get the guts to give him an order? I held my breath, thinking it was the end. But much to my surprise—and maybe his as well—instead of killing me, he bared his teeth like a wolf. And I instantly snapped the shot. Since there was only black and white photography at that time, I worked hard on his portrait, carefully tinting his face with natural skin tones, and making sure that his uniform, medals and ribbons were the right colors. He must have been satisfied with the portraits, because I was allowed to live.

Soon there was another roundup, and once again we were counted, and then sent back to the ghetto. This time most of the people showed up, but as before, anyone who didn't, was found and executed. The next day, August 13, 1942, as often happened, I was sent to Gestapo headquarters. As usual, I expected to shoot the photos, and then take the film back to my darkroom outside the ghetto for processing. This time, however, something very different happened. I wasn't given any film to process, and I was ordered to leave my camera with them. This signaled to me that I was no longer needed. And if there was no use for me, then my life had no value to them. Furthermore, if they didn't need me to take pictures, it probably meant that very soon, there would be nothing to take pictures of.

On a deep, unconscious level, I understood that the ghetto was about to be liquidated. My parents, however, didn't understand when I tried to explain what I thought was coming. Having lost their home and everything they had possessed, they saw me as a naive teenager who was upset that her camera had been confiscated. They didn't sense the deeper implication of the loss of that camera. I felt as if I was disappointing them by insisting that the end was coming. And so we all just went to bed that night. And somehow—I still don't know how—I fell asleep. When I woke up early the next morning, everyone except for my sister and her two little children was gone. The Germans again had ordered all the Jews to assemble. My sister was taking longer because she had decided that maybe I was right, and that we were all about to die. She thought that if this was the case, that the children should be in clean clothes . . . so that there would at least be some honor and dignity in this catastrophe.

When the children were dressed, we rushed to the square where everyone was gathered, and I tried to join my family. But instead, I was pulled aside by a German who pushed me in another direction. Despite my hysterical screaming and begging, I was not allowed to join my family. In the barely controlled chaos, I saw the German official whose portrait I had made. I ran up to him, begging him to let me die with my family, but he just gestured for the soldier to take me away. Why was I being singled out? Prodding me along with his rifle, the soldier took me to the synagogue. Once inside, I saw a few other Jews who had also been pulled away from the others. There were twenty-six of us, and it was with great horror that we realized we'd been spared only because we had skills that the Germans would need in the next few days. I climbed up to the attic and peeked through a small window to see what was happening. I tried to keep my eyes glued to my family. This time instead of just being counted and sent back, they were led to three long trenches, where they all fell after being shot.

The next day, I was called to German headquarters to develop the photos they had taken. Before my eyes, appearing like phantoms on the photo paper, I again saw the heinous deaths of my neighbors, my friends . . . and my own precious family. One thousand eight hundred and fifty innocent Jewish men, women and children. In a trance, I developed the film, and somehow had the presence of mind to also make an extra set of prints for myself. Not that I would ever want to look at them. I didn't expect to live long enough. And at that point, I didn't care about living or dying. I felt guilty for being alive when my family had been killed. But I wanted to leave a record for history.

The Germans soon sent me a Ukrainian girl named Marisha, supposedly to train to be my "assistant," so I knew my days were numbered. During the two weeks that we worked together, I took as much time as I could, taught her as little as possible, and even misled her when I could. And little by little, I managed to hide more film and supplies to use if I was able to escape. I kept postponing running away because I didn't want to be the cause of the other twenty-five "useful" Jews being executed. There soon came a moment, however, when escaping would no longer be my decision—nor my responsibility.

On a dark night in September 1942, a fierce group of Soviet partisans attacked Lenin, turning the streets into a thundering, blazing, and bloody warzone. In the midst of this pandemonium, a young partisan pounded on our door—shouting for us to run to the forest. Somehow the partisans had known about us being spared by the Germans, and instructed him to find us, and tell us to escape. So now we could run to the forest without feeling guilty for endangering each other. And I did. I ran like a mad woman—through flying bullets, explosions, and streets filled with corpses. I ran out of town and into the forest—determined not to stop until I found the partisans.

Totally exhausted, scratched up, and panic-stricken, I finally found them and begged the commander, Misha Gerasimov, to take me. As a young woman, without training or a weapon, I realized that the partisans probably wouldn't want me, and I was terrified that I'd be left on my own in the forest. So I was shocked that he already knew who I was. He also knew that I was a photographer, and that the Germans had kept me alive in order to document their atrocities. Plus, he knew that my brother-in-law had been a doctor, so he decided that I would be able to function as a nurse. Furthermore because of my many languages and fluent Russian, I would be very useful. And with my light hair, it wasn't immediately obvious that I was a Jew, so at least for a while, I wouldn't be a target of anti-Semitism. I was profoundly relieved and grateful that they agreed to take me, and I was determined that I would never make them sorry that they did.

I was able to rest a bit, but it wasn't long before we had to get moving. The hours of walking over rough terrain and through muddy swamps that came up over my knees, took a toll on me. My shoes had disintegrated, and I was now barefoot, but I was wearing a coat—and even though it wasn't leopard fur, it did help to keep me warm. It soon became apparent that the small horse pulling a wagonload of injured partisans, had become weak, and was sweating profusely. If the horse broke down, we would have to physically pull the wagon and carry the wounded, and our progress would be severely hampered. The struggling horse needed a warm blanket—which we didn't have. So I offered to give my coat to cover the horse. I hoped that by doing this, I would be seen by the partisans as being of value—that they'd be glad they kept me. And in fact, a young Gentile partisan, who had heard that I'd given up my coat, later brought me a pair of sturdy, black leather boots that he had taken off a dead German. Instead of being way too big, the boots accommodated my swollen and bleeding feet. These boots would help to keep me alive. When it finally was time for us to stop and sleep, someone gave my coat back to me. And although it was damp and horribly smelly from the horse, I wasn't as cold as I might have been. And somehow, I felt safe. So among strangers, I fell asleep on the ground, under a tree in the forest, wearing a German's boots, and a damp, smelly coat.

The next morning, I woke up with a new sense of purpose. And even a strange sense of hope. I decided that instead of feeling guilty for being alive, that I had been spared for a reason. Now, I was no longer a victim—a helpless prisoner. I was a "citizen" of a vast, hidden world of fiercely defiant partisans,[32] hiding in the forests, daring and determined to fight the Germans. I was a proud young Jewish female partisan. There was again honor and dignity in our lives. Yes, my life was in constant danger, but now I was a fighter. I even had a gun. And I had learned how to maintain it, and use it. I could protect myself and others. And like all partisans, I also had a grenade with which to blow myself up if captured, so I wouldn't break under torture, putting my group in jeopardy. I could now avenge the deaths of my family, which had become my

32. Of the estimated two hundred thousand partisans, at least ten percent were Jews.

reason to go on living. Since I had nothing to lose, there was nothing to be afraid of, and nothing to hold me back.

It turns out that I had joined the Molotava Brigade, which included almost two thousand partisans, from many different backgrounds and circumstances. At that time, only eight of us were women. In addition to combat, there were tasks that women were particularly good at. We could get around without causing as much suspicion as men, so we were good scouts and messengers. Women were also good at operating the radios and decoding messages. Many of the doctors in the partisans were women. And except for some instances of anti-Semitism, all of us, men and women, were very close.

Our territory was the dense forest that lay between Lenin and the city of Pinsk. At that time there were five other brigades in the area with similar numbers. We all were in communication with each other, as well as with Soviet headquarters in Moscow. Because of its strategic location as the Germans' gateway to the Soviet Union, many of our raids were on my home village of Lenin. During the twenty-two months that I was with the partisans, I joined in every possible kind of fight. From small, hit-and-run guerilla attacks, to ambushing Germans and anyone helping them, to destroying roads and bridges. We paid particular attention to the destruction of the train tracks that were essential for German transports of food, weapons, soldiers and eventually, the deportation of Jews to extermination camps. We were dauntless in committing any act that would distract, inhibit or prevent the Germans and their collaborators from carrying out their plans. And the women were as brave and fierce as the men. They had been brutalized and had seen their own families murdered. They had nothing to lose. They were committed to vengeance. And we didn't expect special treatment. During our time in the partisans, we never slept in a house, never slept in a bed. Rain or shine. Winter or summer.

You might be surprised to learn that the summers were actually much worse than the winters. The hot months gave us two additional life-threatening problems. One was that we had to deal with the swamps that took up so much of the forests. We carried heavy weapons and equipment, as well as our sick and wounded. When we couldn't slog through the swamps, or use logs to cross them, we had to detour around them. Swamps were often linked together—they didn't have nice edges like a lake, so sometimes these detours would add many miles to our journeys, and take us dangerously close to German strongholds. Furthermore, since the lengthy detours would also take precious time away from our treks to scheduled raids, there was the danger that by the time we arrived, it would be too late to be effective. Maybe the Germans would have already left—or maybe their numbers would have been reinforced by additional troops, and we'd be vastly outnumbered.

The other big problem with summer was the lack of drinkable water. Dehydration could cause death. Plus, I needed water for medical purposes, and developing film. The swamp water that was all around us was filled with diseases. So we either had to dig for safe water, or hope to find puddles from a recent rainfall. When we dug for the water, it was muddy, and filled with bugs, worms, and disease-causing bacteria. If we were lucky and found a puddle from a recent rainfall, while it was somewhat cleaner and not filled with mud and debris, the bugs and worms were still there. Since I was a nurse and carried woven bandages with me, I came up with a good idea. I stretched strips of gauze bandages across the opening of my hat, and made it like a strainer to drink through. It must have worked ok, because I never got sick.

Surprisingly, the brutally cold winters, when it got to be forty below zero, and often brought blinding storms that practically knocked us over, were better than the summers. This is because we always had access to safe water. No matter how cold it got, we could always eat snow—it was new and clean and free of bugs. Also, we could use it to make little shelters. And because the ground was completely frozen and covered with snow, we didn't have to worry about making detours around the swamps. We could walk right over them. Sometimes we didn't even know that we were on a swamp. After we'd been camped for a few days in what had seemed like a perfect spot, we woke up to find the weather had warmed up enough for snow to start melting. We were in the middle of a swamp. And what was even worse, as we looked around, we were horrified to realize that the swamp contained quicksand, and we were sinking. If we didn't get out fast, we'd disappear, or be perfect targets for the Germans who were getting closer. Fortunately, we managed to get our patients and all of our equipment out in time. So yes, the winters were better than summers—especially when the snow didn't melt.

No matter what season it was, the endlessly dark, dense, and swampy forest was a busy place. In fact, for centuries the forest had sheltered people who were on the run for any of a variety of reasons, so there was a long history of humans hiding, and even living, there. In addition to the many Jews who were now in the forest, there also were hermits who had lived there for years, as well as criminals, roving bandits, spies, and bounty hunters. And while we usually couldn't see more than ten or twenty feet around us, we always knew that there were others around. And since they weren't all friendly, we were always in danger. It was eerie. All these mysterious people slinking around through the forest. You never knew who would cross your path. And someone who helped us on one particular day, could end up denouncing or killing us the next day.

Since most partisan groups were organized strictly for combat, they only accepted people who were combat-worthy and had weapons. There were other camps, including Jewish family camps—that weren't specifically designed for fighting. These accepted people of all ages, and conditions, and were usually in desperate straits, since whatever food, medicine, and weapons they might have had, were easily stolen from them. Whenever possible, we tried to help them. One of the most famous Jewish family camps was created and run by the famous Bielski brothers. Theirs was a unique group in that it was geared both for combating Germans, and for keeping Jews alive. They accepted entire Jewish families, so people of all ages had a place of refuge. Their camp existed in the forest for almost three years. It was a well-hidden, well-run, bustling community that included almost every aspect of a typical village. The people slept in dugouts known as *zemlyankas*. There were structures for a kitchen, a bathhouse, a workshop, a school, a synagogue, a commissary, and a clinic. There was a police force, a court, and a jail. The people had cows for meat and milk and chickens for eggs, and the occasional chicken soup, and some wheat and vegetables were grown. And when needed, many who were able-bodied, volunteered to help other partisan groups in their combat missions. The Bielski commando groups inflicted great damage on the Germans and their collaborators, so the Germans offered large rewards for their capture or death. Despite this incentive, however, the Bielski brothers were not turned in, and because of them, over twelve hundred Jews survived the war.

So there I was, a combat-fighter with absolutely no combat training, who was terrified of guns. Similarly, with absolutely no medical training, and seriously handicapped by my fear of blood, I became a nurse. I had no choice. In Russian, there is an expression that means, "If you can't, we will teach you. If you don't want to, we will force you." So I had to quickly get over my deficiencies and learn whatever I could while I worked. In addition to medical treatment, I tried to comfort those who were in pain and petrified by the shots being fired around them. I was very lucky to be guided by our camp doctor, Ivan Vasilievich, who was really a veterinarian. Despite being a Soviet, he was not against Jews. He appreciated my dedication and ability to learn fast, and he taught me many important lessons about healing . . . and about surviving. In fact, he saved my life several times.

On one occasion, I had unknowingly been put on our group's "hit list," because someone had decided that I had hung on to a few pieces of gold jewelry for my own use. This was strictly against the rules. It was also untrue. Anyone joining the partisans had to give them all their worldly goods to be shared communally or traded for weapons. Doctor Vasilievich convinced the commander that I was not in possession of any valuables, and furthermore, that I was an honorable, effective person, who was of great value to the partisans. So I was no longer under suspicion. I understood that in any group there would be some individuals who could not be trusted. And I was grateful that despite our many differences, with minor exceptions, some of which were due to anti-Semitism, we partisans were very close. Even though we hadn't had the luxury of choosing each other or our living circumstances, and there was no guarantee that a person was trustworthy or even mentally sound, we were unconditionally committed to each other, and to our group as a whole. We lived together, ate together, sometimes sang, danced, and laughed together. We fought Germans together, and raided villages for food and weapons. We took care of each other. And all too often, we died together. The bonds that tied us together were uniquely deep, and forever unbreakable.

Whenever our group went out on a raid, we had several specific goals. One, of course, was to kill as many Germans and their collaborators as possible. Another was to confiscate whatever food, medicine, clothing, and any other essential supplies we could find. As the photographer, I also had another goal: I had to find film, photo-developing chemicals, and paper. So in between shooting and blowing things up, I made side trips to find these precious items. Soon after I joined the partisans, a raid was scheduled that was very personal to me. It was going to be the first attack on Lenin since I had joined the partisans. Even though the commander suggested that I not participate in this one, I insisted on going. This was because in addition to killing Germans, and seizing food and weapons, I was determined get into my darkroom and gather whatever film, photography equipment, and chemical supplies might still be there. I also hoped to find the photographs that I had hidden while I worked for the Germans. This mission also meant that if there were Germans now living in my house, I'd have to deal with them.

With several hundred partisans involved, our raid had to be carefully planned. We were divided up into smaller groups, each with its own target, including the German headquarters and the houses where Germans now lived. We walked all night, carrying our weapons, ammunition, and explosives. Arriving in Lenin just before dawn, and maintaining strict silence, we were able to occupy our positions throughout the town before the sun came up. When everything was ready, the order to attack suddenly came. We instantly blasted our weapons and dynamite, and screamed at the top of our lungs, creating waves of percussive and deafening pandemonium. The abruptly awakened Germans were surprised and confused, but managed to return some fire, before retreating for a little while. It was hard for them to comprehend that they'd been so viciously attacked by what they'd considered to be a raggedy bunch of inferior terrorists.

During the lull, when I was able to get into my house, I was greatly relieved to find it empty. But I soon was furious and frustrated to find that my darkroom also was empty. I quickly put my thoughts together and realized that my former "assistant," Marisha, had undoubtedly taken my equipment. Maybe she still had it, or knew where it was. It was probably crazy, but I was determined to find out, so I decided to go to the house where Marisha had lived. Two of my partisan friends were kind enough to go with me. But before we could leave my house, we knew that we would have to burn it down so that the Germans couldn't use it. My two comrades told me I could leave first and they would light the fire, but I decided that since it was my house, that it was my responsibility. So I said, "Burn it!" And we set my beautiful childhood home, and all its memories on fire. We watched it burn for a few short minutes and then made our way to Marisha's house, having no idea what would confront us there.

When we arrived, we were astounded to see that my possessions had been neatly packed in several boxes, and placed out on the sidewalk. Everything was just sitting there. Apparently someone in the house had figured out that I'd be in on this partisan raid, and in the chaos of a war zone, took a chance on helping me. If the Nazis had found the boxes, my anonymous helper would have been killed. This was incredible! In the midst of the unimaginable, it's hard to single out one particular occurrence as being strange. And finding the boxes was definitely strange. But what happened next was even stranger. As my friends and I picked up the boxes, a woman walked by—just as if she habitually took a walk just after dawn, during a break in fierce fighting. And as she passed by, she handed me my leopard fur coat and hat. And kept on walking.

Even now when I think about it, it's almost comical. No one could make this up. There we stood on a residential street, three young, bedraggled partisans, during a break in a war action, already loaded with weapons and ammunition, lifting boxes of photography equipment and family photos, that had been mysteriously left for me to find, and then, a mystery lady who somehow knew who I was, comes out of nowhere, walks by, and gives me the beautiful leopard coat and hat that the Germans had taken from me a

Partisan Faye Lazebnik

year before. And this coat and hat would save my life by keeping me from freezing. On more than one morning, I woke up with it frozen to the ground—but I was warm and dry. It became like a protective friend to me.

Another prize I was able to obtain on that raid, however, didn't turn out as I'd hoped. We desperately needed clean bandages. They could only be cleaned, boiled, and reused so often before they fell apart. I'd been reduced to washing leaves to put on patients' wounds. So I was thrilled to find a brand new box of bandages in what must have been a Nazi clinic. I couldn't wait to get back to our camp and put clean, new dressings on my patients' wounds. When I got back, however, I got a bad surprise. I quickly realized they weren't the usual strips of gauze. They were, in fact, bandages for casts. This means that once they got wet, they quickly dried hard as a rock. I couldn't use them for a bullet wound or a lacerated leg. So I tried to wash the hardening-chemicals out. I washed and washed and washed, but since I had no rubber gloves, I ended up rubbing all my skin off. I had been so intent on making these bandages soft, that I wasn't paying attention to my own hands. And when I wasn't washing the bandages, I was treating my wounded patients, many of whom had infections. So unfortunately, within a couple of days, my hands got infected. From the tips of my fingers to my shoulders, everything was swollen. The infection spread quickly. And then I got a temperature. I knew I would soon die if I didn't do something. But what?

Well, I finally started thinking that since I was so good at helping others, since I was saving so many lives, since I was taking good care of so many partisans—would it maybe be ok to also take care of myself? And I decided, yes, it would be ok. Because if I didn't get well, I wouldn't be able to help anyone else. So in the middle of the night, with only a little moonlight to show me the way, I went to my Red Cross box, took out a sharp knife, and washed it with alcohol. Actually it wasn't really alcohol. It was the strong "vodka" that the partisans made themselves. And then by the light of the moon, I saw, and knew, exactly what I had to do. I had to stab myself so the pus would be able to leak out. But I couldn't make myself do it. Thoughts crashed through my brain: "You have to have the guts to do it! If you don't, you know you'll die. Don't be a coward! Others need you! Do it now!" So I stabbed myself. The infected pus spurted out. I got weak and must have passed out. I don't know how long it took, how long I slept, but when I woke up, the temperature was gone, and the swelling was gone. So I managed not to die.

That's when I realized how important it was to take good care of myself—that it wasn't selfish of me to do so. The partisans needed me. And in order to stay healthy, I had to keep myself and my clothes clean. Especially from the lice that carried the deadly typhus. And this was not easy. None of us were clean, and our clothes were filthy. As a nurse, however, I had an unusual opportunity to keep myself clean. Since I was always short of bandages, I had to wash, boil and reuse them. I also had to take off the patients' clothes and wash them before putting them back on. Everything had to be washed and boiled for ten minutes. This meant that sometimes I had to go for miles to find water. There wasn't enough water to do this for everyone, so in secret, when I washed the dirty bandages and patients' clothing, I also washed and boiled my own. And I cleaned myself as well. So I was clean. I had no lice. I never had even a cold. My goal hadn't been my own comfort or survival, so much as it had been to be able to save the lives of partisans. That way they could continue to fight.

When I think about it now, it's interesting to me that two of my biggest jobs with the partisans were the complete opposite of each other. On one hand, I had to heal the sick and wounded. On the other hand, I had to kill Germans and their collaborators. I also had to find medical and photographic supplies on our raids, because my third job was to take photos that would document the truth of what the Germans and the partisans were doing. It was quite strange to be taking photos in the middle of a battle. Sometimes I would shoot my gun and then shoot a picture. During surgeries—which were always outside, and sometimes even under enemy fire, I would set up my camera on a tripod, or a big rock—whatever was handy—and either take the photo myself or run back to the patient and have someone else push the camera's button.

Over my almost two years in the partisans, I took over one hundred photos. In addition to the documentary photos, I also did personal photos for the other partisans. They appreciated what I was doing, and tried to help and protect me whenever possible. It wasn't easy making photos in the forest. There wasn't a store to buy film or developer. I had to steal the ingredients for the film developer whenever we raided villages. After taking the photos, I would have to process the exposed film in a makeshift darkroom under blankets. Then, at night, by the light of campfires or the sun during the day, I held photo paper next to the film, so that light could go through it, and in that way, create prints. I still remember how to make my developer. How could I forget? The negatives had to be washed over and over. To this day, they are still in perfect condition. I could never have imagined that sixty years later, those photos would become a beautiful and renowned educational exhibit, sponsored by the Jewish Partisan Education Foundation. My photos now travel all over the world, and are viewed and appreciated by thousands of people.[33]

Along with all my other jobs, I unexpectedly ended up with one more, after another raid on Lenin. We were just leaving the village to go back to the woods, when I was approached by a Christian woman. She was the Greek Orthodox priest's wife, but since the Soviets had arrested him for preaching about God, and sent him to Siberia, she'd been on her own since even before the Germans came. The Germans believed that some of Lenin's residents were helping the partisans, so they were punishing the whole town. The woman had been hiding and taking care of an eight-year-old, orphaned Jewish girl. When all the Jews in the village were being rounded up and killed, the girl's parents had managed to leave her at the church with a note begging the woman to please save her. The girl's name was Raika. And now, the woman was going to try to escape from Lenin. Since she couldn't take Raika along, she asked me to take her with me to the forest.

So there I was. So grateful that the partisans had taken me in. So honored to work night and day with patients, and go on raids. The last thing I wanted to do was cause a problem for them. I didn't have the right to add to their burdens. I definitely didn't have the right to bring a Jewish child—one that I don't even know—into the situation. Plus, I was just a teenager, myself! What did I know about taking care of a little girl? What on earth should I do? Well, what choice did I have? So I went to my commander and told him the girl's story.

And as I'd feared, he became angry with me, really laying down the law, "Faye, this is not a kindergarten. We are fighters. How can an eight-year-old

---

33. "Pictures of Resistance: The Wartime Photographs of Jewish Partisan Faye Schulman" is a traveling photo exhibit produced by the *Jewish Partisan Education Foundation*. This rare collection of Faye Schulman's images captures the "camaraderie, horror and loss, bravery and triumph of the ragtag, tough partisans—some Jewish, some not—who fought the Germans and their collaborators." For information go to www.jewishpartisans.org

survive here? She'll slow us down and be a danger to all of us." So then, I don't know what got into me—but images of my beloved sisters and little brothers, along with all the other children who would never have a life, filled my head and heart. I felt I had a duty to make sure that yet another child didn't lose the chance to live. So I just started to beg him, "Please she will be my responsibility—I will take care of her." Of course I had no idea what I was talking about, or what I was really offering to take on. I just knew I wasn't going to let this little girl die. So I kept on begging. Me, the strong, tough partisan fighter, the nurse who saved lives—the Jewish girl who'd ordered a Nazi to smile, was begging. And no matter what I said, he said, "No, no, and no." Until, out of nowhere, he finally said, "Yes." I think I nagged him so much he agreed, just to shut me up and get rid of me. He had more important things to do.

Well, I'd like to be able to make this sound like a sweet fairy tale, where I was the fairy god-sister who rescued the little girl, and we had wonderful adventures in the forest. But this was reality, and there were many, many challenges. Starting with the fact that the other partisans were very unhappy with me for taking her on. It created an additional mouth to feed and additional danger. And they made their resentment clear. Plus, unlike any eight-year-old I'd ever known, Raika had never had a normal life . . . she hadn't been to school. Everyone she knew and loved had been murdered. She had been given away to a Christian woman. And now—now she was living with a teenager in a wild forest with a bunch of fierce partisans. Plus, little Raika, who didn't talk much, had a mind of her own. She would wander off. Each time she disappeared, the partisans were afraid she'd been captured by Germans or collaborators, and forced to tell our location. Worse, some in our group were convinced that Raika was spying for the Germans. In fact, instead of calling her by her name, they called her "the spy." They wanted to find and kill her. And since I was the one who brought her along, they figured I was also a spy, so now they wanted to kill me. But again, I was fortunate—and once again the doctor took care of the problem. He gave his personal guarantee that I wasn't a spy, and he said he needed me. So Raika and I were saved.

One day, our group was notified that a plane from the Soviet Union would soon be coming to pick up all the wounded partisans, in order to evacuate them to a hospital in Moscow. This was good news because it would allow us to spend more time on raids. The commander put me in charge of organizing, and then moving, the patients along with whatever medical equipment they needed, closer to where the plane was expected to land. It was the dead of winter, and the weather was miserable. I knew that it would take a few weeks for us to get to, and set up, the new camp, and I didn't want to leave Raika alone with the partisans. Furthermore, I thought maybe I could talk the plane's pilot into taking her along with them to Moscow. So I asked permission to take Raika with me, and my commander instantly agreed, saying that it would be a "good way to get rid of her." We trudged through the snowy forest for three weeks before finding the correct location to wait for the Soviet plane.

We set up camp, and tended to the patients, hoping that they would live long enough to get to be rescued. But weeks passed, and the plane didn't come. And in fact, some of our patients actually recovered and went back to our base camp. We were growing more and more concerned. And desperate. During this time, some other partisans passed by, and of course, they noticed and asked about Raika. When I told them about her, it turned out that they knew her uncle. In fact, he was a partisan in another brigade—which wasn't very far away. They agreed that on their way back to their base, they'd try to find him to let him know about his niece. And they did! The uncle soon came to us, and it was an emotional reunion. They were overjoyed to see each other, and he was very grateful to me for saving her life. They were the only two survivors from their entire family. I told him that I had been happy to do it, and now it was his turn to take over. He was very young, maybe eighteen, and I was only seventeen—and here we were, trying to arrange for the life of an eight-year-old. He didn't know what to do. But he told me that his group's location was extremely dangerous—they never knew from one hour to the next what would happen. There was no way that Raika could survive with him, and he had to go back immediately—his commander had not wanted him to leave. So once again, there really was no choice, and I kept Raika.

By that time, we had been away from our base camp for almost six weeks. In my absence, my group had been engaged in many battles, and now needed me back to nurse the newly wounded. So I had to go back, leaving my patients on their own, to wait for the Soviet plane. And I also left without Raika, hoping that the plane would come while I was gone, and that they wouldn't leave her there by herself. Well, a few days after I'd left, when the plane still didn't come, little Raika, this quiet, haunted, eight-year-old child, decided she would go to her uncle. All she knew was the name of his brigade. So all by herself, she made her way through the forest—twenty miles—until she finally got to his camp. What she found, however, was not good. They had just been attacked, and the surviving partisans were stunned to see this grimy, scratched up, lost little girl wander into their camp. When she asked for her uncle, they told her that he'd been killed. She couldn't stay with them, so somehow, she made her way back to our group of wounded, and stayed with them until the plane finally came. And the pilot allowed Raika to join the transport to Moscow.

How do I know this? How could this kind of information possibly be communicated under our circumstances? Well, one of my evacuated patients had been with the Soviet military before being captured by the Germans. When he escaped from the German POW camp, he ran to the forest and joined my brigade, where he'd been injured, and eventually evacuated. In

Faye, bottom row, third from right, is the only female in her group of partisans. To her left, is her Red Cross box.

Moscow, when he recovered, he was naturally ordered to rejoin the Soviet military. Instead, he chose to desert, and come back to us in the forest! He chose to return to the partisans. He found us, and as soon as I saw him, I begged for information about Raika. He told me that a Soviet family was now taking care of her, and that she was safe and well. I had grown to love that little girl, and have never stopped wondering what happened to her. She had been through so much horror. I hope life was finally kind to her.

I have one more story that I want to tell you about brave Jewish fighters. Especially females. For almost seventy years, whenever I speak about the Holocaust, I make sure to tell this story. There was a Jewish girl, who along with ten Russian soldiers, had escaped from a German prison camp, and joined the partisans. One day they were sent to scout out the area for Germans. On the way, however, they were ambushed by Germans who started shooting at them. The Russians turned around and started to run away. They hadn't been sent to fight—they'd been sent to scout! But the Jewish girl stood still and started to scream at them, "COWARDS! STOP! DON'T RUN! WHAT KIND OF MEN ARE YOU? LET'S FIGHT BACK!" And you might find it hard to believe, but they all stopped running. They turned around, started shooting, and ended up killing all the Germans. Then they continued their scouting mission. She was so brave. In German-occupied territory, a young Jewish girl stopped big, tough, Russian soldiers from running away from danger.

I later learned that she survived until liberation, but that some German soldiers, who were returning home, spotted her and killed her. She was already free. And got killed anyway. The war was over and they still had to kill a Jewish girl. Whenever I hear that the Jews went silently "like sheep to the slaughter," I am infuriated to know there are so many stories like hers that will never be told. And even though I'm only one person, I will never stop telling her story, or the stories of the other countless other Jewish heroes who never stopped fighting the Germans. I also know that many of the Jews who survived, did so because of Gentiles who helped them. So I never fail to tell about the Gentiles who helped us. They were also heroes.

The human ability to adapt to circumstances is amazing. The bizarre life I had been leading for over two years had actually become routine. Always being out in the weather, always being on the alert, never being safe, never being comfortable, nursing the sick, the scared, and horribly wounded, watching people die—all of this seemed perfectly normal. This was the only life I knew.

I never even thought about a "regular" life. What would really have been bizarre, would have been thinking about having a family and a home—with
furniture and food. A bath! It would have felt like science fiction to think
about going to a café, and then to the theater with friends. I never planned
beyond the next few hours, so why would I even think of some vague future?
But eventually, the Soviets did push the Germans back, and on July 3, 1944,
our region was liberated. For the first time since July 1941, there was no need
for partisan fighters in our part of Eastern Europe.

At first we were ecstatic beyond belief—laughing and crying with joy! As
we marched into Minsk, we were greeted as heroes, with parades, and bands,
and flowers. The Soviet government made a big ceremony and awarded me a
prestigious medal for heroism. Then we were officially demobilized, and that
was when, for us Jewish partisans, reality sunk in. Our Soviet comrades were
making plans to go home. They would be welcomed back by their families.
They would pick their lives up where they'd left off. Their time in the forest
would eventually become a memory to them.

For the Jews, however, it was a completely different story. We had no
homes—no families waiting for us. Most of our neighborhoods had been
wiped off the face of the earth. Where were we supposed to go? What were
we supposed to do? We had no lives to pick up. We had nothing. How could
we continue living, when so many others didn't? If I ate an egg, I'd see the
one precious egg my mother had carefully split between my sister's little ones
a few weeks before they were murdered. If I stopped by a playground where
children were playing, I'd see the ghosts other children . . . murdered Jewish
children. There were no simple, normal events. Every innocent thing I would
see or do, came with a parallel, and excruciatingly painful memory. And even
more eerie, was the fact that there weren't Jews in this city that had been filled
with a thriving and vibrant Jewish community for centuries. The lives of the
Gentiles in Minsk had returned to "normal." It was as if the Holocaust hadn't
happened. As if the almost fifty thousand former Jewish residents of Minsk—
doctors, lawyers, rabbis, dentists, teachers, students, entertainers, artists, musicians, writers, merchants, tailors, bakers, friends, and neighbors, young and
old—plus the nearly one hundred thousand who had ended up in the ghetto,
had never existed.

I tried to adapt to this regular, "normal" life. But there was no place for
me in a normal world. What was "normal" for me, was living stealthily in the

forest . . . going on raids with my combat unit . . . killing Germans . . . stealing supplies . . . nursing the wounded . . . and taking photographs to document what the world would never believe. Since the war wasn't yet over in Western Europe, many partisans who felt the same as I did, either joined the Soviet military, or the partisan groups that were still fighting in Yugoslavia, Italy, and France. So, I decided the only thing for me to do would be to join another partisan group. At that time, the Soviets were parachuting partisans and supplies into Yugoslavia. This seemed "normal" to me, so I went to sign up. On the way to their headquarters, however, something strange happened.

Outside the Soviet office, a middle-aged officer started to talk with me. He seemed to be Jewish, and I think that he recognized me as a Jewish girl. Almost as if he were my uncle, he expressed interest in my well-being, and I felt completely comfortable with him. He asked all about where I was from, what I had been doing, and what my plans were now. When I told him, he got very serious. He said that since I was all alone, and didn't have anyone to advise me, that he would give me some advice. He knew that if I took it, that I'd always be glad that I did. He told me that I'd done enough fighting. That I deserved to have a life. He said that I had an important skill, and talent as a photographer, and that there was still much important work that I could do in this capacity. So there I was, so close to signing my life away in order to continue fighting as a partisan, and because of this one kind man—a stranger—I just changed my mind. And despite having absolutely no idea how to do it, I decided to try living my life again. And yes, he was right.

Instead of parachuting into Yugoslavia, I took a job that the Soviets offered me as a photographer for the largest daily newspaper—the *Bialoruskaja Pravda*—in Pinsk. When I moved there, even though the authorities offered me my own house, I rented a small room—what would I do with a whole house? I was used to sleeping on the ground in the forest. It was an excellent job photographing post-war Eastern Europe, and I was treated as a VIP wherever I went. But since I was the only photographer in the whole region, and more importantly, since there was no Jewish community, I was very lonely. I also felt unsafe living under the often anti-Semitic, communist rule. So I began to plan for my ultimate goal: moving to Palestine.

Before I could leave Poland, however, I was determined to find out if my brothers, Kopel and Moishe, were still alive. My boss gave me permission to travel, but travel was very restricted. I had to sneak onto trains that were reserved for the military, sometimes hiding from officials who were checking identities. When I told fellow passengers that I'd been a partisan fighter and a nurse, they helped protect me. The word "partisan" brought me respect and gratitude wherever I went. When I finally got to the village where Kopel's partisan unit had been, I was upset to find out that he'd just enlisted in the Soviet military and been sent to the front line. Apparently he had felt the same way as I had about "normal" life. So I made my way back to Pinsk, and started planning a search for my brother, Moishe.

In late fall of 1944, since Pinsk was out of photography supplies, I decided to go back to Minsk, where I knew there was a large supply. I'd also heard that Moishe might be alive and living there. And since he was a photographer, he would probably be working for the Soviets, so I figured he'd be easy for me to find. As soon as I got to Minsk, I went to the Soviets and asked them if they had an official photographer. Not only did they have one, but it was Moishe! And they had his address. So as if it was the most normal thing in the world, I walked over to my brother's apartment building, found his door, and without knocking, just walked right in! I saw him working at a big table in the middle of the room, and my heart almost leaped out of my body! When he looked up at me, a flood of emotions washed over his face: surprise . . . shock . . . confusion . . . recognition . . . and then . . . pure joy.

When we finally recovered from our initial emotions, we started talking about our family, checking if either of us knew of survivors. Sadly, he told me that there was only one survivor from Lenin. It was a man, who I'd known only slightly, but had found very attractive. I was overjoyed to learn that he had been a respected partisan commander, and was very much alive. I was ecstatic to learn that he was my brother's roommate. And soon, I was stunned, when he walked through the door and into the apartment. Handsome Morris Schulman was a few years older than I, and had been an accountant, as well as an officer in the Polish army before the war. He was dignified, brave and very accomplished — especially at blowing up German trains. Whenever anyone had "complimented" him by saying that he "fought like a Pole," he would respond by telling them that he was a Jew, and that Jews could also fight.

Although it took a few weeks for Morris and I to admit it, we knew we were made for each other, and had fallen deeply in love. We had a very small wedding in their apartment in Minsk, and then we both had to separate and

Faye and Morris Schulman on their wedding day, December 12, 1944.

get back to work. Eventually, Morris came to Pinsk, and the Soviets provided us a beautiful home to live in. Morris was also given a very good job as an accountant. So we worked hard, were highly respected, well-paid, and had more money and food than we would ever need. We became part of a little Jewish community, and often had groups of Holocaust survivors over for dinners. It was comfortable knowing that we shared the same experiences, emotions, and thoughts. Eventually, we were able to make contact with Kopel, who had been wounded, and we brought him to Pinsk to recover. He would eventually move to Lodz, where he helped establish a *Yeshiva* (Hebrew School).

We were very busy and the months flew by. The war was winding down, and on April 30, 1945, the Soviets occupied Berlin. On May 9, the Germans surrendered. The war was over. While we worked hard to appreciate our new life, it felt as if we were enjoying a banquet in the middle of a cemetery. It was a repulsive feeling. We knew that we had to do something else. Go some-where else. So we decided to give everything up and leave the Soviet Union as soon as possible. Our ultimate goal was to get to Palestine, but we decided that despite the devastation, the anti-Semitism, and the rampant post-war crime, we would first go to Poland. The only things I took were my precious leopard coat and my camera.

It was a difficult, dangerous trip, and after spending a short time in Po-land, we finally comprehended the extent of the catastrophe there. And we knew that there would be no place for Jews in Poland. Even more determined to get to Palestine, where Jews could live in the safety of their own homeland, we joined an organization, *Bricha*, which helped Jews illegally circumvent the British Blockade. Many of the former partisans who smuggled themselves into Palestine, immediately volunteered to fight for the Israeli army in the 1948 War for Israel's independence.

Our plans to get from Poland to Palestine were complicated by commu-nist restrictions on travel. It turned out that we would have to somehow get to West Germany in order to get a visa for Palestine. How ironic that the country that would now help us get to our Jewish homeland, was the same country that almost succeeded in eliminating the Jews of Europe. So Morris and I began our difficult trek across Czechoslovakia and Austria—we had no money or identification papers that were valid outside of the USSR. The many border guards were brutal with us, subjecting us to humiliating searches and interrogations. Our reality was that we were stateless. We had no pass-ports. We were "displaced persons," and didn't belong anywhere. And we weren't wanted anywhere. We ended up in a displaced persons' camp in Landsberg, West Germany, where we stayed for two years. But before we got to the camp, I had a very difficult task to take care of. I had to get rid of my precious leopard coat. Why? Because I could not come from Poland to Ger-many as a penniless, displaced person if I had a leopard fur coat. There were no Jewish girls around, and since the non-Jewish women treated me badly and didn't deserve it, I had no one to give it to. Just like in the partisans, I didn't have time for sentimental emotions. So I rolled it up and threw it in the garbage. After all those years of protecting me, I said goodbye to my coat so that I could move forward with my new life.

In the Landsberg DP camp, we had our own one-room apartment in one of the eighteen two-story buildings. Everyone in our building had been a partisan, so we got along well, and were used to taking action. We quickly formed a veterans' group, whose primary goal was to support the establishment of the free Jewish state of Israel. We started and distributed a magazine called *The Resistance*, and organized pro-Israel demonstrations. We lived simply, eating only what we needed to stay alive, so we could give surplus food to the Germans in exchange for guns. We were part of a large network that found, cleaned, repaired, and smuggled weapons and ammunition to the Jews in Palestine. This was a life that felt comfortable for us. We knew how to live this life.

In January 1946, however, our lives would change. Morris and I welcomed the birth of our beautiful daughter, Susan. Suddenly, we were parents with responsibilities for an innocent new human being. We were no longer free agents, available for dangerous missions, and uncertain living conditions. We realized with mixed emotions, that we needed a more settled life than that which awaited us in Palestine, so we applied to go to any country in the west. Canada was the first one to accept us. So in 1948, that's where we went.

Our new lives in Toronto brought us many challenges. First, we didn't speak much English. Then, since Morris didn't have documents proving that he was a certified accountant, he had to take a series of low-paying jobs as a laborer. I got a job in a factory as a sewing machine operator. Our wonderful son Sidney was born in 1952, so now we had two bright, beautiful children to ensure the future of our family and our people. After several years of hard work and saving our money, we were able to open our own hardware store, which we ran for fifteen years. Then, Morris became a business broker, and was finally able to use his accounting skills. In 1993, after forty-seven years of a beautiful, loving marriage, my Morris passed away. There isn't a day that I don't miss him.

And now, somehow, it's 2014. It's funny how the past doesn't ever go away. You might be interested to learn that ten years ago, I met a woman—she lives right here in my apartment building—who was fascinated by my story. She informed me that the German government was making financial payments to people who could prove they'd worked as unpaid labor for the Germans. This woman knew how the process worked, and after a lot of research, was actually able to find the record of my "employment" by the Germans. She then worked hard on my behalf to get the Germans to approve my application for payments. Finally, to my surprise, the checks started coming . . . and even though it isn't much, and it couldn't possibly make up for what was done to me and the others, at least it's a start. At least there is now a generation of Germans that recognizes what the Germans did, and are trying to do the right thing.

I have never stopped working to make sure that the Holocaust and the lives that were taken are never forgotten. Although I eventually had to give up photography, I finally found the time to use my artistic talent and became an oil painter. My work, most of it related to my partisan experiences, is hung in galleries and museums. I've been on radio, television, and even YouTube. I am featured on the *Yad Vashem*, Jewish Partisan Education Foundation, as well as other Holocaust-related websites. After thinking about it for over fifty years, I finally wrote a book about my experiences: *A Partisan's Memoir: Woman of the Holocaust*, which was published in 1995 by Second Story Press. Since its publication, people from all over the world come to visit me, and to hear my story. I have traveled throughout Canada, the U.S., Europe, and to Israel, where in November 2008, I was an honored guest at the International Lions for Judah Conference in Israel.

Along with two other anti-Nazi resisters, Barbara Rodbell and Shulamit Lack, I am featured in the Public Broadcasting System's award-winning documentary, "Daring to Resist," which was made in 2000, and narrated by Janeane Garofalo. In 2000, I finally stopped saying "no" to Canadian filmmaker Shelley Saywell, and agreed to do a documentary about my life. It was necessary for me to return for the first time to Poland—a place I never wanted to see again. I was very anxious about this trip to the past. But it turned out to be a wonderful experience—as was the entire project and the resulting beautiful film, "Out of the Fire."

Who would ever have thought that I'd survive the Nazis, survive partisan combat, survive a displaced persons' camp in Germany, and then not only go on to have a wonderful life, but in my seventies, I'd go back to Poland with a film crew! While I was there, I met with former partisans that I hadn't seen since we'd left the forest, and we celebrated with a wonderful reunion—once again, we laughed and cried together. And of course, I visited the memorial for Lenin's Jews to light candles and say *Kaddish* for my family and the others who had been murdered.

Recently, the government of Poland sent an official group to interview me for a documentary! When they first contacted me, I got very nervous. What if they had some secret charge against me, and the interview was a set-up?

Fortunately this was not the case. The Polish government is now trying to learn about the Jewish people and the Holocaust.

The work of the extraordinary people at the Jewish Partisan Education Foundation of San Francisco is ensuring that current and future generations will learn the lessons of the Holocaust and the role of the partisans. In addition to creating and sponsoring the traveling exhibit of my photographs, they have developed outstanding education programs, through which hundreds of teachers have been trained to teach about anti-Nazi Resistance. As a result, thousands of students, all over the country, have learned about, and been inspired by, the stories of the partisans. This education is essential to preventing another Holocaust.

Today, at the age of ninety, I have had to cut back on my activities. My greatest joy is in my two wonderful, accomplished children, six precious grandchildren. And whenever possible, as long as I can speak—I will tell the story. To my dying breath . . . I will tell the story.

Faye Schulman
Toronto, Ontario, Canada, 2013

"There will be a world after this . . ."

Chapter 5

Lola (Leiku) Leser Lieber Sclar Schwartz

1923, Munkács, Hungary/Czechoslovakia—Borough Park,
Brooklyn, New York

Lola Leser Lieber
Krakow, Poland, 1939

Lola Lieber Schwartz
Brooklyn, New York, 2012

Entering Brooklyn's Borough Park was like going through a time warp into another world. In this bustling center of American Hasidic Jewish life, the inhabitants' dress and rituals reflect their commitment to a lifestyle that might seem to outsiders as being more 18th century Europe than 21st century New York. The men all wore black coats and brimmed hats. Curled side-locks, known as *payos*, framed their bearded faces. The women wore long skirts, and scarves or wigs covered their hair. The school names on the sides of the bright yellow buses were printed in Hebrew instead of English.

When Lola opened the door to her upper flat, her very modern, attractive appearance presented a stark contrast with her unique community. She swept me up into a warm, enthusiastic, and tearfully happy hug, as if we were long-lost relatives instead of strangers. And I felt the same way. I had waited two years for this hug. Even though Lola and I had never met in person, we weren't total strangers. This is because I had read her beautiful memoir, *THERE WILL BE A WORLD AFTER THIS: A STORY OF LOSS AND REDEMPTION*. I had also been very fortunate to work with Lola's brother, Ben Lesser, as the editor of his remarkable memoir, *LIVING A LIFE THAT MATTERS: From Nazi Nightmare to American Dream*. And through the eyes of her "little" brother, I grew to know and love Lola before we'd ever met.

I was concerned that since she really didn't know me, that she wouldn't be comfortable with a stranger who already knew so much about her. I didn't want her to feel that her privacy had been breached. Much to my relief, Lola already trusted me, and was happy that we could finally meet. She graciously showed me her elegant, art-filled home, and pointed out her own extraordinary paintings. After chatting briefly, we adjourned to an elaborately set dining table for a luncheon that seemed as endless as it was delicious. Later, sitting together on her outside balcony in the soft summer shade, I listened as Lola told me her story. And, just as with Manya and Faye, I was transported back to Lola's time on the run from Czechoslovakia, to Poland, Hungary, Romania, Austria, and finally, to a DP camp in Germany. Not affiliated with a resistance group—and thus without their protection—Lola, just like thousands of other Jews, "resisted" on her own, in any and every way she could. Whether snatching a sacred Jewish book from under the noses of German guards, to confronting Adolf Eichmann in his Budapest headquarters, Lola put her trust in *Hashem* (Hebrew name for God),and followed her instincts to defy oppression.

Here is Lola's story . . .

Borough Park, Brooklyn, New York, 2012

When you ask most people what country they were born in, they usually don't have a big problem giving you the answer. That's probably because they were born in an actual country, instead of one that had been quickly pieced together like a puzzle, from parts of other countries. Villages and towns, on the other hand, stayed pretty much the same, no matter who was in charge. For example, the country of Czechoslovakia, where I was born in 1923, didn't even exist until 1920. But Munkach, which was the town where I was born, had been in existence for centuries. From the Middle Ages until the end of World War I, Munkach had usually been under the control of the Austro-Hungarian Empire. Amidst changes of governments, the Jews would do their best to adapt and carry on their daily lives as usual. All this changed, of course, when the Germans decided that Germany needed more territory in 1938, and just came in and took over Czechoslovakia. At that time, they also gave the Munkach region back to Hungary. And after the war, there were even more changes, with it ultimately becoming part of Ukraine. So now you can see why it might be easier to tell you which town I am from, than the country.[34]

When I lived in Munkach, it was a vibrant and well-known center of Jewish religion, learning, and politics, and almost half of its approximately 30,000 residents were Jewish. About a quarter of the residents were Ukrainians, and another quarter were Hungarians, so we didn't feel as if we were a minority, and I wasn't aware of anti-Semitism. The overall cultural influence of the region was Hungarian, and my maternal grandparents, who were of

---

34. At the end of 1944, when the Soviets pushed the Germans out, they gave Munkach back to Czechoslovakia for a short time. It then it briefly became part of the Soviet Union, before becoming part of Ukraine.

Polish origin, identified strongly with the Hungarian culture. They were well-off financially, and owned a very large, beautiful home that extended far back from the street. We felt safe and secure behind the tall, wrought-iron fence that surrounded our property, the centerpiece of which was a beautiful, elaborately designed front gate. The extensive property included fruit and nut orchards, flower gardens, and a beautiful glass gazebo that we used for *Sukkot* (an autumn Jewish holiday of thanksgiving). There were also several additional small buildings that housed various domestic employees, including housekeepers, a laundress, a cook, landscapers, a carriage driver, and my strict German governess. It was an oasis of security and beauty, which I considered to be my own personal enchanted garden. And I was delighted to be treated as a princess.

So maybe now you're wondering, why are all these historical details important in a story about Jewish and Gentile Polish women who resisted the Germans? Well, it would turn out that the small detail of my being born in Munkach, when it was in Czechoslovakia, meant that unlike my parents and siblings, I was not a Polish Jew. And this would become critically important following the German invasion of Czechoslovakia's neighbor, Poland, in 1939.

Here's how it happened.

My father's side of the family had lived in Krakow, Poland for generations. This is where he had grown up and created a successful chocolate candy manufacturing business. He was a very loving and religious man, who worked long hours, and was very successful. Like his father and grandfather before him, he was very well-known and highly respected. Similarly, my mother's family, which had lived for generations in Munkach, was also loving, religious, successful, and highly respected. This presented a problem for my newlywed parents. Neither really wanted to move to the other's city. To accommodate my mother and her family, my father did try to run a business in Munkach, but his attempt failed for reasons beyond his control. One reason was that he was not fluent in Hungarian, which was the language of commerce in Munkach. Another reason was that he lacked a broad network of friends, relatives, and business contacts. Furthermore, as a foreigner, he couldn't get a business license. He had no choice but to stay in Krakow. So my parents decided that my mother, and any future children, would go back and forth on a regular basis, essentially splitting their time between Krakow and Munkach. We didn't have bullet trains back then, so the trip took all day by train, and became increasingly difficult as the family grew.

When my mother was pregnant with me, my older brother, Moishe, and older sister, Goldie were already born, and *Mammiko*, as we called her, had her hands full. It was natural that she would want to give birth surrounded by her loving family, who would take good care of her, the new baby, and the other children. So that's how a Jewish girl from a Polish family was born in Czechoslovakia at what would turn out to have been a time of historical importance. My maternal grandparents, who missed having us all with them, doted on me, and my extended visits eventually turned into a permanent residency. Usually, Goldie and my brothers joined us for the summers. It seemed normal for our family to live in these two separate houses, in two separate countries. And although I didn't know it then, this living arrangement, by providing me with the opportunities to become bi-cultural, would later help me not only resist the Nazis, but to survive.

My childhood was filled with love, learning, beauty, fun, and a future that looked bright. I was multilingual, and very artistic. I attended public school and had a tutor for Hebrew. I was also well-educated in the sports, religions, art, music, cultures, and foods of both countries. I was alert to multicultural cues that showed me how others were thinking, and therefore, how they would behave. In just a few years, when the Germans came, my broad education, many interests, and ability to think and function within more than one culture simultaneously, would provide me with essential survival skills. Unlike so many other people, I wasn't frozen in one way of thinking or being. This enabled me to convincingly assume a variety of identities . . . so many, in fact, that sometimes it was hard for me to know if the real Lola was still there.

Looking back, I can see that my life divided into very distinct stages. The first, of course, was my idyllic childhood as a well-loved Jewish child of privilege. This all came to an abrupt end on a crisp fall day in 1938, when I was fifteen. My mother had come to Munkach for the High Holy Days. As was routine for non-Czech citizens, she had checked in with the consulate upon her arrival. This time, however, instead of the usual routine, she was informed that her Polish passport—which included any young children—was no longer valid. She had twenty-four hours to get out of town. In our blissful ignorance, we had not been aware that under the pressure of Nazi Germany's

Lebensraum, long-standing hostilities between Poland and Czechoslovakia were heating up, and so something as simple as crossing this border was now impossible.

I had rushed home from school that afternoon, eager to hug my mother and discuss our family's plans for the holidays. When I saw her ashen face, I was stunned. And when she explained that we had to pack immediately and get back to Krakow, I was unable to comprehend what was happening to us. Just an hour before, my thoughts had been about exciting social activities, pretty clothes, and best of all, enjoying the High Holidays with my family. There was no way for my brain to process the fact that I had to pack immediately so we could get to the train station. We were suddenly, for the first—but far from the last—time, on the run from overpowering and deadly forces we did not understand. As a teenager, this was something that I definitely was not prepared for, and did not want to do. I was leaving everything I knew and loved and was forced to move to a completely different environment. How would I make friends? Would everyone laugh at my poor Polish? Where would I go to school?

So the second stage of my life began without fanfare when, as a young Hungarian teenager, I suddenly had to learn a new way of life. I had to become Polish. Even though our cultures were similar, there were endless subtle differences that would distinguish me as being an outsider—and for a teenage girl, that was to be avoided at all costs! So I worked hard and learned quickly. My first priority was to perfect my Polish, so people would respect me when I spoke. And I especially wanted to go to the very special Bait Yaakov Hebrew Academy for Girls. It was the first approved Hebrew school for girls, and had been founded in Krakow by an amazing woman, Sarah Schenirer. She was a radical for her time because of her belief that Jewish girls should have the same opportunities for a Jewish education as did the boys. At first, I was frustrated because my Hebrew wasn't good enough for me to qualify for admission, but I worked hard, and eventually, I was accepted. I also attended their summer camp, where I was able to enjoy sports and art. One of my challenges however, was that I didn't fit in with the other girls. My stylish clothes and silk stockings contrasted sharply with their more homespun outfits and bulky wool tights. They thought I was a frivolous, spoiled rich girl. When I realized that my appearance was causing people to see me in a negative light, I decided to change my appearance. Soon, I was accepted by the other girls.

Another aspect of my new life included working in a fine corset shop that my aunt owned. She needed help, and felt I was qualified to do the job! I learned fast, worked well with customers, did some sewing, and also handled the cash register. It was exciting to be treated like an adult, and I took my responsibilities very seriously. I was beginning to see myself as a young woman instead of a girl. Adding to this new perspective was that I had met a very interesting man at a family wedding. Since he was eight years older than me, I didn't think of him as a potential suitor, but he was very accomplished, and I was flattered that he seemed interested in talking with me. There was no way to know that by meeting Mechel Lieber that night, my life would change forever. Similarly unknown to me at that time, was the fact that the lives of Europe's Jews were also changing forever. The 1930s were coming to a close, and the Germans were on the move. They quickly occupied Austria in 1938, and since the world didn't seem to notice, they easily took over Czechoslovakia. When they invaded and occupied Poland, in September, 1939, the next stage of my life had begun—and I hadn't even known it was coming. It's funny how history happens while people are just living their lives.

It wasn't long before I would have my first exposure to the Germans. It was a beautiful autumn day, and when I looked through my living room window, I saw a priest walking alone down the street. Because of my interest in fashion as well as other religions, I was fascinated by his elaborate robes. When he lifted his arms to the sky, I was comforted to imagine he was praying for peace. With teenage sentimentality, I felt joy to know that everyone in Poland was pulling together despite our differences. As quickly as the thought entered my mind, however, it was shattered by an explosion unlike anything I'd ever heard or felt before. Our house, and everything in it, shook. The sky turned black. When the air finally had cleared enough, I could see that a bomb had destroyed a building just down the street. It turned out that the "priest" had been a German spy, whose mission had been to confirm the location, which been the headquarters for an anti-German newspaper, should be destroyed. His pious arm-raising had given the bomber the "ok" signal.

Soon, Krakow was filled with German soldiers, whose distinctively tailored uniforms, and tall, shiny, black leather boots always signaled danger. And my family would learn first hand of their utter lack of humanity. One night a group of Germans barged into our apartment, brandishing their weapons, shouting obscenities at us, pushing us around, and demanding our valuables. While everyone rushed around trying to gather jewelry and money to give them, I was ordered to go to my parents' bedroom with one of them. He slammed the door shut and attacked me, but for some reason, instead of becoming paralyzed with fear, I surprised myself by fighting him back. Miraculously, at the very last minute, I was saved. The other Germans wanted to leave, so they broke through the door to get him. This experience taught me the importance of actual physical fighting—something that was totally the opposite of how I'd been brought up.

So I quickly went from being a protected young Hungarian Jewish child, to a Polish Jewish teenager who went to school and worked, to being an unprotected target of mass-murderers—and who knew she could fight. For those of us who had been brought up with strict religious and cultural guidelines about proper living, this terrifying new world, with no guidelines, made it impossible for most of us to think ahead or make any plans. In Krakow, there as yet was no "resistance." It was all happening too fast, and people clung to their belief that it would soon be over. But the only thing that happened "soon" were the endless directives we had to follow. First, each Jewish home was marked with a Jewish Star so that everyone would know where the Jews lived. Next, all Jewish businesses were "Aryanized," meaning that they were taken over by Gentiles. Jewish business owners were required to stay on for a couple of weeks to train the Gentiles who had taken over. My father derived some comfort however, from the fact that he had been saving for "a rainy day" ever since the Germans took over Austria. As a result, he had accumulated quite a bit of money, and it was in American dollars. Even with his foresight, however, he wasn't able to prepare for what came next.

The Germans soon forced all Jews over twelve years of age to wear armbands with yellow Jewish Stars. Children were no longer to attend school, and able-bodied Jews were forced to become slave laborers. Every morning, the Germans would send flatbed trucks up and down the streets, pick up anyone they wanted, and then take them to work in factories, farms, and construction sites. Many of these laborers would never be seen again. During these days, my girlfriends and I typically passed the time by meeting at each other's houses, trying to create a sense of normalcy. We chattered about clothes, did each other's hair and made plans for falling in love. Unfortunately, Jews were not allowed to gather in groups, and on a day when I hadn't joined my girlfriends, they were discovered and taken away. From that point, the descent of Krakow's Jews into hell was quick and unobstructed. In May 1940, we were confronted with a so-called "choice": We could take whatever we could carry and move into the recently formed, overcrowded Krakow Ghetto, or we could take what we could pile into a horse and cart, and move to the country. Since we didn't have anywhere in the country to move to, neither way provided us any hope.

But help arrived from an unexpected source. Mechel Lieber, who had been visiting us on a regular basis since we'd met at my cousin's wedding, came to speak with my father. He told him that he loved me and wanted me to be his wife. As my father was recovering from the shock of this grown man wanting to marry his fifteen-year-old daughter in the middle of a catastrophe, Mechel continued talking. His father, Herschel Lieber, had been very successful, and managed to hide a considerable amount of money and valuables. Instead of going into the ghetto, the Liebers were planning to leave Krakow and move to a small nearby village named Niepolomice. Mechel wanted my family to join them. He offered to handle all the details, even finding us a place to live close to his family. My father realized that we had no choice, so he agreed. Suddenly, we would once again be leaving a beautiful, comfortable home and heading off into the unknown. And with the knowledge that an interesting man wanted to marry me, another stage of my life had begun.

We packed as much as we could onto the horse and cart, taking only what was absolutely the most practical for our new lives. That meant that certain things that we loved had to be left behind. My parents seemed to be arguing about the bags of religious books that my father wanted to take. My mother felt that there were more important things to take, such as blankets and warm clothes. This made my two younger brothers and me nervous because our parents never argued. Uncharacteristically, however, my father insisted, and the books were added to the growing collection of possessions in our cart. We headed out of town, hoping that we wouldn't be stopped.

After only a few miles, however, our worst fear appeared ahead of us. It was a German checkpoint. They were stopping and searching all the Jews that were leaving town. They took whatever caught their eye, particularly Jewish books, which they heaved on top of a huge pile. To our horror, they immediately grabbed the bags containing my father's books, and threw them on the pile. Bad as this was, more terrifying to us was our father's face. It lost all color. He looked like it was the end of the world. When we asked him why, he told us that he had carefully hidden all his American dollars in between the pages of those books. We now had nothing.

Hearing this, and much to my family's shock and horror, I instantly ran up to one of the Germans and begged him to let me keep some of my father's books, telling him that my father was a writer. My unthinking defiance could have caused me and my family to be killed. Maybe the German thought he'd have some fun with me before killing me, because he told me to go ahead and grab the books from the pile. He had known that these thousands of sacred books all looked alike in their brown and black leather covers. He knew that I wouldn't be able to climb up the shifting pile to where my father's books had landed. I tried, but before I could find any belonging to my father, the German told me that my time was up, and I had to leave. While I was grateful that I hadn't been killed, I was crestfallen that I let my father down, so again I was defiant. I grabbed the closest book and ran back to my family. It wasn't my father's, but I felt triumphant that at least we would still have one Jewish book. I had once again stood up to a German. Having fought against both the German attacker in our Krakow home, and then confronting the German as we left town, I started to acquire a new sense of being proactive instead of being a victim. This new view of myself would be very helpful when things looked hopeless. Holding our breath, and praying to *Hashem* to protect us, we resumed our journey down the road.

When we finally arrived at our new "home," we were shocked to see that it was an ancient, thatched-roof, mud hut. It was divided into two one-room residences, one for the landlord and one for us. There was very little furniture, and lacked indoor plumbing. We had no idea how our family could live in such a place. But under the circumstances, we had no choice, and we were grateful to Mechel for all his hard work in finding us the place. We knew that he had saved us. And as the weeks went by, we tried to settle into a routine. My resourceful father created a little pretzel-baking business so he could generate a small income. Mechel and I continued to see each other, and soon, I realized that I loved him. When we talked about the future that we probably would never see, Mechel let me know how important it was that we get married. We had no idea how much longer any of us would live, and he wanted us to spend as much time together as possible. Naturally, all I could think about was how miserable it would be to have a wedding in this awful place, where it was forbidden for Jews to gather in a group, where we weren't allowed into the synagogue, where I wouldn't have a bridal gown, and where we had no food. But Mechel said that we weren't going to let the circumstances stop us. And when my father gave us his blessing, he promised me the best wedding I could imagine just as soon as the war was over.

So we did it. On August 5, 1941, with the help of our brave and loving family and friends, we managed to put together a little wedding in the backyard of the synagogue. If our bittersweet gathering had been discovered, we would all have been killed instantly. And tragically, as it turned out, of the twenty guests who risked their lives to celebrate our marriage that day, only three, including Mechel and I, would be alive in 1945. I was only seventeen on my wedding day, and by nightfall, overwhelmed with mixed emotions, I cried for most of my wedding night. My wise husband, however, spoke softly to me, and helped me to see things as a grown woman, "Lola, be strong. We will survive . . . there will be a world after this." Those words became the theme for the rest of my life. No matter what I was faced with, I knew I would survive.

Lola and Mechel Lieber's wedding
Niepolomice, Poland August 5, 1941

Mechel had a Gentile friend who happened to be the mayor of Niepolomice. He also had an extra room in his home, which he rented to us. After a
few short weeks, he warned us that the Germans were coming soon. At that
time, my parents and two younger brothers had gone to the town of Plaszow,
near Krakow, to visit with my older brother Moishe and his wife, Frieda.
While this was a terribly dangerous thing to do, my mother insisted on seeing
them. So at least they would not be in Niepolomice for the Germans. Mechel
worked on a plan to get me and his family out of town, but with thousands
of Jews on the move throughout Eastern Europe, this was a difficult task.
And then, disaster struck. Early one morning, the Germans took my father-
in-law, along with a truckload of other men to the forest. We would later
learn that they had been executed. Heartbroken, my mother-in-law was persuaded to go to the Bochnia Ghetto, where she would live in a small house
with her three daughters, and a grandchild.

Our friend, the mayor, told us that a pogrom was coming, and that we
needed to run. Mechel and I piled on all the clothes we could, and tried to
look like peasants. This was easier for me than for Mechel, because I had
blond hair and blue eyes, and could pass as a Gentile. Mechel's appearance,
mannerisms and speech were obviously Jewish. It was important to spend as
little time as possible out in public. We were helped by the mayor, who in the
middle of the night, and risking his own life, drove us to the train station.
Having no other choice, we were heading to the notorious Bochnia Ghetto,
where Mechel's mother was now living with three of her daughters and a
granddaughter. This was a dangerous destination as the Germans there were
known for their butchery. At that point, however, we were buying a few more
hours of life—we didn't have the luxury to plan for whole days.

When we arrived, we quickly found the ghetto—which the Germans had
deliberately established near the train station, in order to expedite deporta-
tions to concentration camps. We found Mechel's sister's little house—and
even though it was overcrowded, she welcomed us warmly. In the midst of the
hunger, disease, humiliating regulations, and bleak future, our family was
strengthened by the presence of the revered and beloved Rabbi Shloime Halberstam, who was famous as the Bobover Rabbi. The presence of the rabbi and
his family inspired us to resist the Germans—even if our only resistance was the
refusal to die. And for some Bochnia Ghetto residents, resistance would soon
become more than just the refusal to die. It would become active combat.

Organized Jewish resistance in Bochnia had begun with typical social and work groups that had already been in existence, such as labor unionists, train conductors, Zionists, socialists, communists, and scouting groups. Many of these included both Jews and Gentiles. They were used to working together for common goals, and had the skills, as well as the communication networks, that were necessary to actively resist the Germans. Religious communities joined together to try to help whoever needed it the most. Sometimes, kind Gentiles were able to sneak us food through the ghetto fence. Even though we traded items for the food, they were still taking a terrible risk. And at that point, their families were also starving, so it didn't feel like they were taking advantage of us. We each traded what we had for what we could get. Heroic secret couriers, who worked for the resistance, darted in and out of ghettos throughout Eastern Europe transporting false identification papers, food ration cards, money, and personal letters to relatives. They were our connection with the outside world—as well as with our families who were trapped elsewhere. There was a hopeful energy in the air.

This energy was soon put to the test when an *aktion* came. Thousands of Jews were killed or taken to the Belzec camp, where they were exterminated. The time had come for us to take action. People started building hiding places behind walls and under chicken coops and dog houses. This was a slow process because if their actions had been seen, they would have been executed. The Germans offered rewards to anyone who denounced, caught, or killed a Jew. We were encouraged, however, when the *Judenrat* put Rabbi Halberstam in charge of ghetto's Hygiene Committee. This kept him relatively safe, and it allowed him access to official letterhead and most importantly, typewriters—items that would soon become very useful.

Our family had decided to dig a large bunker in the backyard under the woodshed. Its entrance would be camouflaged by covering it with the chicken coop. It was a complicated task, and everyone helped. Fortunately, we weren't far from a frozen pond. In the middle of the night, as we each dug the bunker, we'd fill a pail with dirt, and then creep to the frozen pond and pour the dirt through carefully concealed holes into the water below. Once our bunker was dug, we "furnished" it with blankets and whatever food and medicines could be safely stored. We had done a good job, and our bunker was imperceptible. And we finished it just in time. All too soon, the Germans came. We rushed to the bunker with Mechel's mother, sisters, and niece. There would be barely enough room for us to squeeze in. At the last minute, a man and two women appeared. He told us that if we didn't let the women into the bunker, that he would denounce us. We didn't have time to resolve this situation, so after a brief argument with Mechel's mother and youngest sister, who insisted that we go into the bunker and leave them to the Germans, Mechel and I helped them all into the bunker and covered it with the chicken coop. There was no way we could have lived with ourselves if we had lived at the expense of his mother and sister.

So there we were, a young married couple, holding hands as we wandered around aimlessly on the last night of our lives. Out of nowhere appeared a Jewish policeman, named Farber. He was horrified to see us out on the streets, instead of in hiding. After we explained what had happened, he took a great risk by giving us directions to where his sister and her two small children were hiding. It was a small water tank on the roof of a leather-tanning factory. When we found it, we climbed up and into the tank, quietly explaining to the policeman's terrified sister that he had sent us. Mechel and I each then took a heavily sedated, sleeping child to hold so the mother could rest her arms. We were standing in almost two feet of icy water, and we could feel the slimy coats of water rats that swam through our legs, occasionally taking little bites.

We stood there all night. And all the next day. And another night. Periodically we could hear Germans and their dogs outside, so we stood perfectly still, and never said a word to each other. Eventually, we heard what we hoped was Farber's "all-clear" knock. And slowly, with swollen and stiffened arms, hands, and legs and feet, covered with cuts, we climbed out of the water tank. I could barely walk. Farber took us back to his house so we could warm up. With his face devoid of all color, and lips so tight that they barely moved, he sadly told us that many had died in the *aktion*. He told us he'd seen bodies near our bunker. Mechel and I knew what we had to do. So in the middle of the night, we left the policeman's house and walked through the snow to the bunker. On the way, we saw a small cart, which we brought along. We knew we might need it to take bodies to the cemetery.

Our worst fears were confirmed when we got to the bunker and saw the bodies of Mechel's mother, sisters, and little niece. Mechel somehow managed to control his own emotions—and mine. As I swallowed my silent screams, he held me and told me we couldn't waste time—our relatives must be buried. We carefully and lovingly lifted each one and placed her on the cart. As we were leaving we spotted one of the shovels we'd used to build the bunker, and took it with us. We were grateful that it was still dark, because burying Jews was prohibited, and we would have been shot. When we arrived at the Jewish cemetery, we proceeded to dig one grave big enough for all of them. It was grueling work. We didn't have gloves, and our fingers froze. When we finally had placed our last precious relative in the grave and covered it with dirt, we hid the cart and the shovel and sadly said goodbye. Walking home, I suddenly lost my barely controlled composure when I realized that we had not said *Kaddish*, the prayer for the dead. There was no other choice. Despite the hints of daylight, we rushed back to the cemetery, and the grave, and said *Kaddish*. No matter what the Germans did to our bodies, they would never break our souls. They would never make us forsake the religion that had sustained us for thousands of years.

During the next few days, Mechel and I were in terrifyingly uncharted territory. Physically, our continued existence was in doubt. Emotionally, we were drained. Mentally, since nothing like this had ever happened before, we had no way of knowing how to proceed. Mechel was a highly intelligent, responsible son, brother, and husband, who was dealing with the loss of his father, mother, sisters, and niece, as well as his determination to keep his young wife safe. He was committed to the peaceful world we would one day inhabit. I, having been abruptly moved from girlhood to womanhood, was trying to figure out how to be a wife, and a partner, as well as a fighter for our future. In the midst of this confusion, without any notice, and just as if they hadn't been in another village many miles away, my parents arrived. They brought my two younger brothers, my older brother Moishe, and his wife, Frieda. They had heard about the *aktion* and were determined to find us. As overjoyed as we were to all be together, we were almost paralyzed with fear about what was coming. We had seen new posters directing all Jews to report to the *Judenrat* the next morning. The Germans wanted to count the survivors. So we would be registered and given new identity cards.

The next morning, we all lined up outside the *Judenrat* office where a young clerk was registering us. When it came to my turn, I gave him my name, date of birth, and in response to his query about where I was born, I replied, "Munkach, Czechoslovakia." This got the immediate attention of an older officer named Schoenblum, who came up and asked me to repeat what I'd said. Which I did. Then there was a long silence during which time, I held my breath and listened to my pounding heart. What he finally said filled me with terror: "She doesn't need an identity card. Bring her to my office at nine tomorrow morning." We all knew what this meant: German officers routinely selected attractive young Jewish women to become their personal entertainment, usually killing them when they were no longer useful. There was no question in my mind that I would die before submitting to a German. My family and I walked back to the house as if in a trance.

After a sleepless night, with all of us holding on to each other, two Jewish policemen knocked on our door and told us that it was time for me to go. We all walked to the ghetto gates together, and then I went through the gate with the policemen. I could see how badly they felt, how horrified they were to be delivering me to the Germans. When we arrived at the former Jewish home that was now German headquarters, I had to proceed on my own to Schoenblum's office. As if my brain and body separated, I somehow walked into his office. And then something very strange happened.

This important German offered me a chair, and in a regular speaking voice, embarked upon a normal conversation with me about where I was from. The very "normalcy" of this conversation was horrifyingly *abnormal*. What kind of game was he playing? For some reason, he focused on Hungarian topics, asking if I spoke Hungarian—which I did fluently. And specific popular Hungarian songs, with which I was very familiar. We chatted about goulash and other Hungarian delicacies. Eventually, he stood up and my heart stopped beating. But instead of molesting me, he said in a very fatherly manner, "Lola, you are a very lucky young woman. You are clearly not a Polish Jew. You are Hungarian-Czech. You are, therefore, exempt from the requirement to live in the ghetto." Then he tore off my Jewish Star armband, and told me that I was free to leave the ghetto.

I'll never know how I managed to process this astounding turn of events, but while thanking him profusely, I dared to mention that I wasn't alone. That I couldn't possibly leave without my husband and family. I assured him that they all had also been born in Munkach. Instead of screaming at me for being an ungrateful Jew, he thought for a moment, and then told me to bring them to his office the next morning. And he instructed his secretary to provide new identification papers for all of us. I was almost delirious with gratitude and spontaneously kissed his hand—something that typically would have caused my instant death. I almost floated out of his office and out to the street. I was surprised to see that the two Jewish policemen had waited for me—hoping in spite of their fears, that I would come out. When they recovered from the shock of seeing me so happy, they escorted me back to the ghetto, where we were greeted by a joyous eruption of pandemonium. I was gathered up in hugs as happy tears streamed down the faces of Jews who hadn't had anything to be happy about in many years! One of our own had survived a meeting with the Gestapo chief. This was a miracle. My family covered me with kisses, danced with joy, and lifted me above their heads as we made our way back to our house. Even the Bobover Rabbi came with us, telling me that I was a hero—like Queen Esther—because I was saving the Jews. I had no idea what he meant, and was embarrassed to receive such praise.

That night, the rabbi and one of his students visited us to discuss their plan to obtain false identity papers for other Jews. As the head of the Hygiene Committee, he had access to official stationary and a typewriter. His student had the unusual ability to carve reverse letters and numbers on rubber-balls which could be covered with ink—thereby making a variety of "official" stamps. Since we were now were in possession of authentic identity papers, we could use them as templates for a document forgery operation. And that's exactly what we did. Starting that very night. We set up a forgery operation in our basement. My brother, Moishe, was an exceedingly talent artist, and able to make authentic-looking documents. Also artistic, I joined him in this process. Everyone helped in some way, and to our delight, we turned out thirteen documents, including birth certificates, for Hungary and Czechoslovakia. We were lucky that my knowledge of the languages allowed me to write the correct words. Among the new documents were identification papers for the Bobover Rabbi and his family. That's why he had likened me to Queen Esther. He'd felt that my actions had made it possible for him and his family to escape, thereby ensuring the continuation of the historic Bobover dynasty.*

---

*They eventually were able to reestablish the Bobover Dynasty in Borough Park, Brooklyn, New York—where I also have lived for the last almost sixty years. Until he passed away in 2005, he never failed to thank me for "saving the Bobover Dynasty."

Finally free to leave the ghetto, we moved into a small apartment, and the Rabbi and his family found one close by. We continued our forgery operation while making plans to escape to Hungary. Of course we weren't the only Jews trying to get out of Poland and go to Hungary. It turns out that underground partnerships between Jews and Polish Gentiles had developed for just this purpose. The process involved the use of coal trucks with false bottoms. Yes, the drivers were paid, but since they and their families would be executed for their actions, I don't think they all were exploiting desperate Jews for the money. Many were brave Christian men who were saving Jewish lives. And because of them, many Jewish lives were saved. Fortunately, the Rabbi and my husband were able to make contact with a coal truck driver who agreed, for a price, to hide us in a false bottom of his truck. He would take us to the edge of the High Tatras mountains which separated Poland and Hungarian-controlled Slovakia. Then we would proceed on foot to the top of the mountain, where we would find a Gentile woodsman. This woodsman would guide us down to the bottom where we would cross the border. And be free.

This seemed like a crazy dream. We had no money to pay a driver, and we had no idea how to cross mountains on foot. But since it was the only option, we started making plans. A wealthy family who'd been in contact with the Rabbi and Mechel, decided that they also wanted to escape in a coal truck. So between them, they struck up a deal. They agreed to cover the costs if Mechel handled the details. Part of the deal was that our family would be allowed to go along. Of course, since the Germans made it worthwhile for Gentiles to turn Jews in, there was no guarantee that the driver could be trusted. Even if the driver was an honorable man, there was no guarantee that the truck would make the trip without being caught, in which case, he'd be executed along with his passengers. Furthermore, since there was only room for seven in the truck, and the wealthy family had first priority, there would have to be three trips. It was decided that Mechel and I would go first, along with five members of the sponsoring family. If we survived, the others would follow.

One night, just as it seemed that our outlandish plan was all set, a group of Germans barged into our apartment, and dragged Mechel and I, as well as Moishe and Frieda off to jail. When we got there, we saw that the jail cells were filled with other prisoners. Some were criminals, some were prostitutes, and several of them were friends of ours who had also been involved in the forgery operation. We knew that we'd been denounced, and that we'd be tortured to provide the names of others. This was clearly the end. Suddenly, amidst the crying, screaming, moaning, praying, and even raucous singing of the other inmates, Mechel and I, along with our friends, were freed. Apparently one of the other Jewish prisoners had been able to bribe the guards. To our horror, however, Moishe and Frieda were not so lucky. They were sent to different concentration camps.[35]

As soon as we returned home, we finalized our escape plans, and within a few days, it was time to go. We made our way through a blinding rainstorm to the vacant lot where the truck was waiting for us. All seven of us somehow managed to squeeze into the tiny hidden compartment, where we lay side-by-side on our stomachs, drenched and trembling. The truck shook as the coal was loaded on top of us. Nauseated by the lack of air, along with the smell of wet clothes, sweat, dirt, coal, and exhaust fumes, I had to concentrate on not being sick. After traveling for a few miles, we were abruptly stopped by Germans who ordered the driver to unload all the coal. When this task was complete, they stomped all over the truck's floor, making holes with sharp spikes. At any moment any of us could have been stabbed by the spikes. We struggled not to cough or sneeze from the coal dust that covered us. Miraculously, we were not discovered. The driver reloaded the coal, and we continued to our destination. After we made our painful exit from our cramped compartment, he wished us well, and told us how to find a guide's cottage at the top. Then he dumped his load of coal, and left us at the bottom of the mountain.

We were not in good shape. We were cold, our muscles ached, and we couldn't walk on the rain-soaked ground. The only way we could climb the mountain was on all fours, like animals. One of the wealthy men was older, and frail. He begged us to leave him to die on the mountain, but we refused, and half-carried, half-dragged him along. Somehow, we managed to get to the top, and found the woodsman's cottage. His wife had prepared a hot meal for us, and we were grateful to warm up by the fire and rest for a while before continuing our journey. We set out before dawn, and then divided into two groups as we approached the border guards. Mechel and I and one other

35. We would learn many years later that Frieda had survived the camps, and Moishe had actually managed to escape, but ironically, and tragically, he was soon killed in an Allied bombing attack.

person went first, trying to look like a cheerful group of Gentile Czechoslova-kians who were on our way to Hungary. If we were stopped, I would do all the talking since I was the only one who spoke both languages. Fortunately, we weren't stopped. We got through and found a place nearby to sit and wait for the others. Tragically, when they came across the border, they somehow aroused suspicion. They were stopped, and turned over to the Germans. How strange that while their money saved us, it hadn't been able to save them.

Here is an example of the active, extensive, and heroic network of Jews who had dedicated their lives to saving other Jews. My mother's brother Beri had left his home and family a year previously to set up a way station near the Hungarian-controlled Slovakian border with Poland, in order to help Jews who were sneaking out of Poland and into Hungary. We were among the many Jews who survived because of his efforts. He met us in town and took us to his house, where we rested for a while before heading on to Budapest. When we got there, we were shocked to see the healthy looking residents—Jewish and Gentile—conducting their lives normally, as if they weren't sur-rounded by war and the genocide of the Jewish people. Within the space of two days, we had gone from a ghetto that was about to be liquidated, to a filthy, cramped compartment in a coal truck, to a rain-soaked mountain, across a dangerous border, and now, much to our disbelief, we were actually checking into a hotel. There would be a real bed and clean sheets! Further-more, although we were in the Jewish Quarter, it was a bustling neighbor-hood, not a squalid, guarded ghetto. We even had our meals in a kosher restaurant there. Even stranger than our sudden "normalcy," however, were the reactions of the Hungarian Jews when we told them about what was go-ing on in Poland. We were stunned that they did not believe us. They thought we were exaggerating. Nothing we said had any impact on them. They confi-dently told us that such a catastrophe could never happen in Hungary.

After a few days of rest and recuperation, we were thrilled to be reunited with my younger brothers, Ben and Tuli, who had survived the same trip in the coal truck, and had come over the mountain, just as we had. Two young boys—Ben just fourteen, and Tuli barely eight—can you imagine their fear and their courage? My heart almost leapt out of my body when they walked through our door, with big grins on their faces. And we held on to each other for dear life. They could only visit us briefly before going with our uncle to Munkach. Our joy, however, was soon darkened by our worry about my parents. Why hadn't we heard from them? Fearing the worst, Mechel and I decided that instead of waiting and worrying, since Munkach was only a few hours away, we should go there to visit my grandparents.

So without wasting any time, we embarked upon a journey to my beloved home. It was almost as if we had to do everything as quickly as possible because there was no way of knowing what was coming next. Our anxiety about what we would find in Munkach was alleviated when we arrived and were smothered by the hugs and kisses of my grandparents, uncles, aunts, cousins, my sister, Goldie, and brothers Ben and Tuli. Overjoyed to spend time with each other, we were afraid to speak about what had happened to Moishe and Frieda. We were afraid to even think about why my parents still hadn't arrived from Bochnia.

Despite the beauty, serenity and love provided by my grandparents' home, Mechel and I could see signs that Jews would not be safe for long in Munkach. We had seen these signs before, and knew all too well what they meant. Mechel and I also knew that our identity documents wouldn't protect us in Munkach once the Germans came, so we would have to return to Budapest. We held a family meeting to try and make a plan. We told everyone what had been happening in Poland. Ben and Tuli, who also had experienced the horror, tried their best to convince them. But just like the Jews in Budapest, my family either didn't believe us, or didn't agree that running was the best option. We begged them to join us, but they refused. They wouldn't let Ben and Tuli go, and of course, Goldie refused to go without the others. Agonized by their decision, Mechel and I returned to Budapest alone. And soon thereafter, just as we'd feared, my cherished family was swept up and deported to Auschwitz. Only much later would I find that Ben had somehow survived.

Upon our return to Budapest, we saw that it was teeming with all kinds of refugees. It seemed as if there were more refugees there than the original Budapest residents. In fact, all of Hungary was teeming with refugees, because as the last country to be occupied by the Germans, it was the only place refugees could go. It seemed that everyone we saw had run from somewhere else, including Gentile intellectuals, military deserters, many others who were targeted by Germans. Since there were so many of us who needed false identity papers, an extensive and complex black market industry had sprung up to provide these documents, as well as cigarettes and other merchandise that was in high demand.

Our current identities as Polish Jews would no longer protect us, so we decided to become Polish Catholics. Mechel soon made the appropriate contacts, and we became a lovely young Polish Catholic couple. Of course this was easier for me since I not only looked Gentile, but had learned about the Catholic religion. I could mimic Gentile mannerisms, and speech patterns. Mechel, on the other hand, thought, looked, and spoke like a Jew, and knew nothing about Catholicism. He would have to stay in our tiny apartment as much as possible to avoid being denounced. For the first time, we were able to spend a few days together, enjoying each other's company. Then, because our apartment was too expensive, we decided to move one-hundred and twenty miles east of Budapest, to the town of Debrecen. I had many relatives there, and felt its location near what had once been the Romanian border, might be helpful at some point.

So we boarded a train and set off for yet a new destination. Upon our arrival, we were relieved to find a Jewish landlady who agreed to rent us a room—even after we introduced ourselves as Michael Nowakowski and Janka Nowakowska, a recently married Catholic couple. Over the next few weeks, we managed to create a routine without drawing attention to ourselves. Since I could easily fit in with the Gentile population, I had many more advantages than Mechel, including mobility, and I didn't feel as trapped as he did. It was like leading two lives. One life was when were alone together in the apartment, or visiting my relatives. The other life was when I was out on the streets as a Polish Catholic. It was confusing and nerve-wracking. Soon Mechel announced that he would no longer hide his Jewishness. He joined up with other Jewish families and started going to *Shul* every morning. When I expressed my fear and frustration with his activities, he explained that it was necessary to belong to a strong network of Jews so that we'd have a support system in case we once again had to hide or run. In fact, he had already worked out an escape plan. He must have had a premonition.

On March 19, 1944, the Germans invaded Hungary. The nightmare had caught up with us again. One night, we heard heavy steps pounding up the stairs. Mechel rushed into the bathroom. Germans broke into our apartment demanding than Michael Nowakowski come with them. With as much composure as I could gather, I explained that my husband and I had had a fight, and he had left the apartment. They demanded that I tell them if he was a

Jew. Putting on the expression of a proud Polish Catholic woman who had just been insulted, I practically sneered my denial. "A Jew? Are you kidding? My husband ran from Poland because he didn't want to fight the Germans." They knew I was lying, and broke into the bathroom. For a moment, I thought that our lives were finished. But the Germans came right out in a fury. The bathroom was empty. Mechel had managed to squeeze out the window, and dropped down two stories into the yard. Unfortunately, he injured his foot and was quickly caught.

And now, with the capture of my husband, a new stage in my life was beginning. I was a woman alone, who was determined to get her husband back. My first goal was to find someone to share my apartment expenses. Luck was with me and I was able to make arrangements for my cousin Rosie and her young daughter, Micheline, to come live with me. They also had blonde hair and blue eyes and were passing as Polish Catholics. Rosie had close friendships with Gentiles, who despite the sacrifices and risks, helped us on many occasions. Rosie, Micheline, and I settled into a daily routine, and I felt strengthened by being part of a family. I decided to find the wives of the other Jewish men who'd been picked up the same night as Mechel. We made contact with each other and were relieved to discover that our husbands were all still in Debrecen's prison. We worked out ways to get packages and secret messages to them. But while the other women stayed focused on making their husbands' lives less miserable in prison, I was devising a plan to rescue Mechel.

A few days later, the prison was bombed by the Soviets, and once again, thinking that Mechel was lost, I felt that my life had ended. We soon discovered, however, that the Germans had moved our husbands to bomb shelters before the attack, and when it was over, moved them to a makeshift outdoor jail on the edge of town. Our husbands were still alive! Now, instead of signaling the end of my life, the Soviet bombing meant that the Germans were being pushed back. I began to believe Mechel's words that "there would be a world after this." And with that hope, I came up with an idea. It's funny how something that's totally outlandish—even insane—can appear to be the only course of action to a desperate woman. And so, without stopping to think about it, I decided to visit my husband in the jail. I borrowed a bicycle and rode to the gate, terrified that at any time I'd be stopped by Germans. Luck was with me again and I got to the prison gate safely. Despite my pleas, the guards would not let me in. They wouldn't even discuss it, and I didn't want to make a scene, so I left.

While the Soviets were attacking Debrecen, the Germans had more important things to think about than a few Jewish prisoners, so the guards became lax. This allowed us to smuggle notes back and forth with our husbands. At one point, Mechel and I were even able to meet very briefly at the jail's fence. The fact that he looked so weak and depressed gave me even more energy and determination to rescue him. But as so often happened, our plans were abruptly thwarted. In April 1944, the men were moved to a more secure prison in Budapest. And all Hungarian Jews were required to move into the nearest ghetto. In their rush to beat the quickly approaching Allies, it would take the Germans only two months—from early May to early July 1944—to liquidate approximately half of Hungary's estimated 825,000 Jews. The Jewish ghetto in Debrecen was soon enclosed by a huge wall. I knew that if there was any chance to save Mechel that I would have to go to Budapest. Rosie refused to let me go alone, and despite the risks, her kind Gentile friend offered to drive her and Micheline to Budapest. There wasn't room for me in his car, so I would take the train. We would meet at the *Judenrat* inside the Budapest Ghetto. This trip would put us in terrible danger for two reasons. One, we were Polish Jews using false papers to pass as Polish Catholics as we traveled to Budapest. Two, we would be—and had to act like—"Polish Catholics" inside a Jewish Ghetto. Since we might look suspicious to anyone who saw us, we weren't safe in either identity.

I arrived at the ghetto just before curfew, and was able to slip inside without being questioned by the guards. The streets were deserted, and I had no idea where to go, so I wandered around until I saw an open door. I ducked inside, and was relieved to see stairs leading down to the basement. I crept partway down the stairs, and that's where I dozed for the next few hours. I was awakened when the door opened and a man demanded to know who I was, and what I was doing there. For some reason, I risked telling him the truth. It turned out that he was part of the *Judenrat*.[36] Not only that, but Rosie and Micheline, who had arrived before me, had also met him, and he had let them sleep in an apartment upstairs! The next morning, we decided

---

36. It might interest you to know that this man was Rezso Kasztner, the highly controversial leader of the Zionist Rescue Committee (ZRC).

that as Polish Catholics, we needed to get out of the ghetto as soon as possible. Fortunately, we were able to find, and quickly move to, a very small apartment, not far from the ghetto.

As I was wracking my brain trying to come up with some scheme for freeing Mechel, I became aware of all the people on the streets. They all looked awful. They looked beaten and hopeless. Their clothes were in tatters. It was a massive group of victims—completely indistinguishable from one another. And then, another crazy idea popped into my head. Instead of blending in, I realized that I needed to stand out. I needed to appear as a mysterious and glamorous woman, who was confident about her plans and activities. Rosie generously gave me what little money she still had, and when I had carefully groomed and dressed myself as elegantly as possible, I walked through the streets, talking with people and gathering information. After just a few days of this masquerade, Rosie got word that we had aroused suspicion in our apartment. So we gathered our few belongings and moved immediately.

This would happen again and again. We'd find a place to stay, then I'd wander the streets as an elegant, important woman, gathering news, then we'd arouse suspicion and have to move with no notice. We'd sold everything we could in order to cover expenses for the room and food as well as the bribes I needed for information. I had come up with a new trick that gave some credibility to our disguises. I'd ask every new landlady if she knew where the closest church was, and what time the services were. I even walked to the church on Sunday mornings. Sometimes I stayed for a while to learn more about the congregation. Other times I just went in the front door and straight out the side door.

I soon found out that a nearby shoemaker's shop was the center of secret Jewish activity. It was like a message center. I'd been able to use it to maintain contact with the wives of the Debrecen prisoners, a few of whom had also come to Budapest. We were allowed to send packages to our husbands every other week, but we were strictly forbidden to include any kind of messages. I got around this by cutting the top off of a Hungarian pepper, hollowing it out, inserting a coded note, and then putting the top back on. Mechel was able to decipher my codes, so we established a primitive communication system. Along with these communications and the information I gathered at the shoemaker's and on the streets, I was surprised to learn that an extremely high-ranking German official had just taken up residence at a villa on the

Buda side of the Danube River. His name was Adolf Eichmann. He was known as the most evil—and most effective of Hitler's henchmen, and he had been sent to personally oversee the liquidation of Hungary's Jews. With nothing more to lose, I decided to speak with Eichmann.

Dressed as beautifully as possible, I went to the gate of his villa, and in my perfect, aristocratic German, informed the guard that Eichmann was expecting me. Without any question, he announced me, and I was admitted. When the receptionist saw me approach, he opened the door and told Eichmann's secretary that I had arrived. As I entered what could end up being the place of my death, my mind flashed back to the entrance of Schoenblum's office outside the Bochnia Ghetto. It seemed like a lifetime ago, and I hoped that Hashem would protect me this time as He had then. Behind the secretary's desk, sunshine streamed through French doors that were open to a patio. Eichmann himself was out on the patio enjoying a cigarette. Tall, handsome, and beautifully attired in his formal German uniform, he turned slightly, looked me over, and motioned me to speak with the secretary. Again in perfect German, I explained all about my Catholic husband, and even threw in the word, "unfair." This word must have caught Eichmann's attention, because he came into the room and asked what was going on. I thought it ironic that this monster didn't want to be associated with the word "unfair."

Face-to-face with Adolf Eichmann, instead of feeling terror, I was struck by how absolutely normal he looked. He could have been a professor or an accountant. There was nothing about him that suggested that he was the human incarnation of evil. This realization would stay with me for the rest of my life. There is no way for us to know from the outside, what is inside the heart and mind of another person. The secretary told him that I was trying to gain information about my husband. I looked directly at Eichmann and told him that my husband was from an important Polish family and that we had escaped to Hungary in order for him to avoid being conscripted to fight against the Germans. Eichmann responded, "Well, there is one way to confirm this woman's story." And he directed his secretary to call the prison. At that moment it dawned on me that my plan was not only foolish, but would ultimately hurt Mechel. I realized that the whole time that secretary was on the phone, Mechel's guards were checking to see if he was circumcised. When the secretary looked up at me with cold eyes, I believed that my plan would cause not only Mechel's death, but mine as well.

Instead of falling apart, however, I managed to put on my coat, thank the secretary for his help, nodded goodbye to Eichmann, and walked out of the office. I wondered how long it would be before German guards grabbed me and either killed me on the spot or sent me off to my death. Maybe Eichmann had let me go because he had been impressed by what is called *chutzpah* in Yiddish, and means, "shameless audacity." Maybe it was divine intervention. Whatever it was, I just kept walking until I got back to our apartment. And while I was recovering from both my shock at surviving, and disgust at my failure, my Mechel was being beaten almost to death in his prison cell.

Hoping that he would live, and that he would be able to forgive me, I continued trying to figure out a way to free him. There was one small factor of encouragement: on July 7, 1944, since the Soviets were closing in, the Germans had stopped deporting the last few remaining Jews, and therefore, Mechel, to extermination camps. With the retreat of the Germans, we were able to keep on hanging on, and my determination to free my husband was given new strength. I had made many contacts throughout the underground community. I was surprised by how many people were working against the Germans. And they came from all walks of life. It might surprise you to learn that the person who helped me rescue Mechel was a Gentile prostitute, who used her German clients as sources for important information that helped Jews.* She put me in touch with a Hungarian doctor who was willing to sign a document indicating that Mechel was mentally ill and needed to be transferred immediately to the hospital in the Budapest Ghetto. This was a very unusual and complicated arrangement, especially since the prison had its own hospital.

Apparently, the doctor was a sympathizer and knew just what to do. I again hollowed out a pepper and stuck in a coded message telling Mechel to act like a lunatic. He figured out the code, and proceeded to do it so well that even his cellmates wanted to get rid of him. So the transfer was made in the middle of the night. Very early in the morning, Rosie, Micheline, and I set off for the ghetto. We had hidden his clothes in a bag of treats for the patient we were supposedly visiting. We got through the ghetto gate and into the

---

*Although many people look down on these women, they often took great risks to gain important information from their "clients," which they then conveyed to partisans, as well as Jews. Many of these women were caught and executed. Many others who managed to survive only ended up suffering horribly after the war for their perceived "collaboration" with the Germans.

hospital without any problems. As we walked through the hallways, we tried to look as if we knew what we were doing, while we desperately searched for Mechel's room. He hadn't even been registered yet, so there was no record of him being there. When we finally found him, there was no time for joy—he had to immediately change clothes and walk out with us. As the only one who spoke Hungarian, I kept up a constant chatter about the "patient" we'd just visited. Mechel, Rosie, and Micheline nodded and grunted appropriately. And to our sheer joy and relief, we got out of the hospital, out of the ghetto, and arrived safely at our apartment.

We lived quietly in our apartment until the war finally ended, and we had to get out of Hungary and the coming Soviet occupation. We embarked upon yet another difficult journey. Our goal was to get to the United States, where we had family. But first, we had to get into Germany, of all places, in order to get visas. Once again we piled on layers of clothes, packed what we could carry, and through all kinds of weather, trudged through the countryside, and crossed mountains. This trip was particularly difficult for me because I was pregnant, and tired easily. I was determined, however, that my miracle-child would be born in safety, so I refused to stop until we arrived at St. Ottilien, a former monastery near Frankfurt that had been turned into a DP camp and hospital.

When we arrived, I was immediately placed in a hospital ward, and against hospital rules, Mechel, as an expectant father, was given a room down the hall. Before separating for the night, we held each other close, thanking *Hashem* that we had survived. We were free. We were safe. We would live with our child in the world that Mechel had foreseen. And I finally was entering a new stage of life that was a blessing! It never occurred to us that we would soon be granted yet another miracle.

One day, my roommate, who was a young teen girl, was visited by two young men. After a lengthy and emotional visit, they said sad goodbyes, and left her with a photograph of the group they all belonged to. When I noticed that one of the boys had the same beautiful curly hair as my brother Ben, I was thrown into a profound sadness that I would never see him again. For some reason, I asked the girl if I could look at the photograph. She was quite insistent that she could not show it to me. This seemed strange to me. Why couldn't she show me a photo? So I also became insistent, and she eventually gave in. It turned out that they were a group of illegal Zionists, who were leaving the next day on a prohibited trip to Palestine. They had trained for months in secrecy for this dangerous mission. Under no circumstances was anyone outside of the group supposed to know anything about it. Her sudden illness prevented her from going with the group, and the boys had come to say goodbye to her.

When I looked at the photo, I thought I was having a hallucination. I had quickly spotted the curly-haired young man, and despite the fact that he was no longer fourteen years old, there was no doubt that he was my brother, Ben. What words could there possibly be to express my emotions at that moment? After all we'd been through, to come to this room, to this girl, with me on the verge of motherhood, and to learn that Ben was not only alive, but had just been in the same room with me! I screamed for Mechel, who of course feared that something terrible had happened, and so practically flew to my room. I told him the wonderful news. I also told him that he had to do whatever was necessary to find my brother and bring him to me immediately—once Ben left for Palestine it would be too late. Mechel knew better than to try to reason with a desperate pregnant woman. He contacted a cousin that we'd recently found, and sent him to search the Frankfurt area.

Incredibly, our cousin found my brother. Of course Ben was stunned first to see his cousin, and then overwhelmed to hear that his sister was alive. He was also placed in a terrible situation. His group was scheduled to leave in the morning. When Ben told his commander he wanted to go see his sister, the commander was infuriated by what he saw as a betrayal of the cause they had worked so hard for. A betrayal of the future state of Israel. After much agonized soul-searching, Ben decided that seeing me was more important than going to Palestine. He changed his whole life so that we could be together.

And so the two cousins took a bus to St. Ottilien. When Ben returned to my hospital room, and our eyes met, he rushed to my bed and swept me into a hug that only ended when we needed to breathe again. We sat together and talked endlessly about what we had been through, and what had happened to our family. Ben told me about the roundup in Munkach and the brutal deaths of our family. I was sickened to hear about the horrors he endured in various concentration camps, as well as on the death march and the death train. In fact, he had been only hours away from death from starvation when the Allies liberated Dachau. Weighing only sixty pounds, he was rescued by a priest, who carried him over his shoulder like a sack of potatoes to St. Ottilien, where it took him six months to recover.

When we were able to talk about other things, we made joyful plans for the new baby and our family's future. Mechel was able to make arrangements for Ben to sleep in his room, so there was no danger of us being separated again. They both stayed with me during the next few days, until I felt some unusual pains, and realized that I was about to become a mother. Our beautiful son was born on January 19, 1946. We named him Hershel, in honor of Mechel's father. As the first Jewish baby in the region, he was treated like royalty—and so were we! Gifts were showered on all of us, and people stood in line to hold him. And everyone who held Heshi commented on his eyes. They were conspicuously wise. Little did we know then that his beautiful eyes foreshadowed the contributions he would later make to the Jewish people.[37]

At that time, in an ironic turn of events, Germans were being forced to give up their homes so that homeless Jewish refugees could live in them. Because of this, we were soon able to move out of St. Ottilien and into a lovely apartment in Munich. It had belonged to a German widow. When we spoke with her, she offered to be our housekeeper if we would let them stay in one of the rooms. Despite how strange this seemed at first, we agreed. Who could ever have imagined that we would be sharing a home with a German woman? Amazingly, we all got along well, and even became like a family. She pampered Ben, and treated baby Heshi as if he were her own grandchild. She cooked and cleaned for us, and we also helped her. Even after we left for the U.S., we stayed in touch with her, and sent her packages.

After a few months, we received our visas to go to America. We bought tickets on the SS *Ernie Pyle*, but much to our frustration, bureaucratic confusion prevented Ben from going with us at that time. On our day of departure, we tearfully had to say goodbye, promising we'd see him as soon as his papers came through. Two weeks later, on February 18, 1947, we arrived in New York, and yet another stage of my life began.

---

37. Hershel has devoted many hours to finding Jewish adults in Poland who survived the Holocaust when they were adopted as children by Gentile families. Many of these people had no idea that they were Jewish. As a result of Heshi's work, there have been hundreds of family reunions.

We were joyously welcomed at Ellis Island by our loving relatives, who had already arranged a small apartment for us in a Jewish neighborhood. Mechel quickly set about making contacts to find work, and ended up peddling women's hosiery. Since silk stockings had not been available during the war, the newly invented nylon stockings were very much in demand. I wanted to come up with a way to make our stockings different, and therefore more desirable than others then on the market. I wanted to decorate each stocking with a small, hand-painted flower or butterfly at the top. Now that I had the idea, I had to figure out how to make the paint flexible so it wouldn't crack when stretched. After much trial and error, I was able to come up with the right formula, and we went into production. These beautifully decorated stockings became very popular, especially after the Can-Can Dancers at the Radio City Music Hall decided that they wanted big roses hand-painted on the knees of their dance tights! We couldn't keep up with the demand, and had to hire several artisans to do the painting. Mechel did well, and we eventually opened our own hosiery business.

And busy as I was, I was determined to become a legitimate fine-art painter, and devoted as much time as possible to developing as an artist. I studied privately with a well-known art teacher until I was ready to start exhibiting my work. Eventually I joined the Woodstock Art Association, in Woodstock, New York, and studied there with John Pike at his Watercolor School, and with the renowned Stefan Lökós at his Studio School and Gallery. During this time, Mechel and I were blessed with two more precious children. Joseph, named after two of his great-grandfathers, was born in 1948. Our daughter Mati, named after Mechel's mother, was born in 1957. The children did well, and brought us great *nachas,* which in Yiddish means "joy." Our joy, however, was not to last. Tragically, in 1958, my beloved husband, Mechel, was diagnosed with cancer. In keeping with his indomitable character, he fought this disease with everything he had, and lived until 1966. The children and I were devastated to lose him. I had no idea how to live a life without him. But hard as it was to face the future, I had to honor his memory by carrying on—into whatever world lay ahead after this one.

What lay ahead, as usual, were new stages of life that I could never have imagined. In 1960, I had opened Lola's Art Gallery in Borough Park, and become a businesswoman in addition to an artist. I couldn't let this business suffer because I was now a widow. I worked hard, and met with success. My paintings can be seen at *Yad Vashem*, the San Francisco Museum of Modern Art, as well as in galleries and private collections. Throughout the years, I have taken on many commissions for portraits. It was in this capacity that I would meet Norman Sclar, the wonderful man who became my second husband. He had read an article in a magazine about my painting portraits on commission, and come into my gallery to meet me. He apparently was impressed by my work, because he hired me to paint his late wife's portrait, then portraits of his two children, and then his own and in the process, we fell in love. In 1967, with our children in attendance, we were married. Norman and I shared fourteen wonderful years before he passed away.

Once again, I faced an uncertain future, but I was blessed to meet Rabbi Shimon Aryeh Schwartz, a well-known and widely-respected writer in both the U.S. and Israel. We married in 1984, and had eleven beautiful years to-gether, before I once again was widowed. I continued with my painting, and to this day, still run my gallery by appointment. Looking back, I thank Hashem for my long, full life, and the blessings I have been granted, includ-ing the love of three remarkable men. My three wonderful children have blessed me with 12 grandchildren, 48 great-grandchildren, and two great-great-grandchildren. They are my personal answer to Hitler's Jewish Ques-tion. They confirm that what Mechel and I did was worthwhile. They are living good Jewish lives, and making valuable contributions to the world that Mechel promised me would come after the Germans.

And now, it's 2014, and I'm ninety years old. This is a stage that no one can prepare for. Other than aches and pains that don't hesitate to remind me, I don't really notice the time that has slipped away. I keep extremely busy with my family, and with so many relatives, someone is always getting mar-ried, having a baby, or a birthday—the most recent of which was a beautiful celebration they all threw for my 90th birthday. That night, when I looked at my precious family, I saw the past as well as the future that Mechel knew would come. He would be very proud of them.

I am also still very involved in the Jewish community and the schools, where I make presentations about the Holocaust. I'm honored that the stu-dents really seem to listen to me, and even care about what I'm saying! My brave and devoted younger brother, Ben, grew up to be a loving, religious, hardworking, and honorable man. In Yiddish, we would call him a mensch. I'm proud of his success in real estate, as well as his non-profit Zachor Holocaust Remembrance Foundation, which provides Holocaust education at no charge to schools and community groups.

Even though Ben now lives in Las Vegas, we remain very close, and speak on the phone several times a week. Despite the distance, I manage to get out to the west coast sometimes, and he comes to New York, so we see each other and each other's families whenever possible. Ben and his beloved wife, Jean, are very close with their two lovely daughters, their four grandchildren and great-grandson.

In 2008, after much urging by my family and friends, I finally sat down and began writing my memoir, *A WORLD AFTER THIS: A MEMOIR OF LOSS AND REDEMPTION*, which was published in 2010. While it was at times painful and frustrating to revisit the past, it was also a cleansing and inspiring experience, and I'm glad that I was able to leave a record that shows what happened. I try to keep up with the times, and am happy to let you know that I even have a website: www.lolalieber.com. I am already busy writing my next book, and hope that by sharing my experiences, my actions will have meaning for others.

I especially want people to know that I was never a hero. In fact, I was usually terrified. And I was sometimes probably even foolish. I was just a regular person who managed, with *Hashem's* help, to defy the Germans in whatever ways I could. My determination to endure was strengthened by my love for my family, my Jewish faith, and my husband's promise that there would be a world where we would live in peace. I never stopped praying that *Hashem* would show me the way. And I have never stopped thanking Him when I am given the strength to do what has to be done—even when it has seemed hopeless. Especially when it has seemed hopeless. I have tried to live my life in a way that honors the blessed memory of those who were lost, as well as the generations that have joined us since, and the generations still to come.

Lola Lieber Schwartz holds her
great-grandson and great-great-
grandson at her 90th birthday
celebration.
Brooklyn, New York 2014

"I was just a little girl, but I knew all of our lives depended on me doing exactly as I was told . . . so that's exactly what I did."

Chapter 6

Miriam Miasnik Brysk

1934, Warsaw, Poland—Ann Arbor, Michigan

Miriam Miasnik
Romania, 1945

Miriam Brysk
Ann Arbor, Michigan, 2013

Driving through the winding, tree-lined roads of Ann Arbor, Michigan, I looked forward to finally meeting Miriam Brysk. During the previous year, I'd had the honor of working as Miriam's editor on both her memoir, *Amidst the Shadows of Trees*, and her Holocaust-Art Education book, *The Stones Weep*. We both were looking forward to our first face-to-face meeting. I turned into the driveway of her beautiful contemporary home, and saw her waving excitedly from the front door. As she greeted me with warm, happy hugs, what struck me immediately were her whimsical smile, and her eyes that held deep secrets. This unique combination provided hints to Miriam's soul.

As we entered her bright, artful home, Miriam introduced me to her husband Henry, who is a retired physicist. We then sat at their kitchen table for refreshments and conversation after which Miriam then set about showing me her astonishing artwork: a cutting-edge combination of computer technology and photography, which brings the viewer an understanding of history within a personal context.

Despite having had her early education postponed by the war until she was twelve years old, Miriam became a university medical school professor. In 1967, she earned her PhD. in Biological Sciences from Columbia University, and went on to a career as a professor of dermatology, microbiology, immunology, and human biological chemistry. She has published eighty scholarly articles. Following retirement, her subsequent incarnation as a highly-respected artist has resulted in her work being displayed at *Yad Vashem*, as well as in numerous galleries and in over twenty-five exhibits. How did the determination and maturity of a little girl, who spent her young years living in bomb shelters, and then lived with the partisans in the Lipiczany Forest, demonstrate resistance to the Germans? Even at the young age of six, Miriam's self-discipline, adaptability, and ability to follow orders displayed a maturity well beyond her years. If she was told to stay silent for hours, that's what she did. If she was told to pretend she wasn't Jewish, that's also what she did. This maturity figured prominently in both her survival, and the survival of those around her. Coupled with her exceptional intellect and determination, Miriam's maturity would facilitate not only her extraordinary recovery from the horror and deprivation of her childhood, but a career as a well-known and highly-respected scientist.

Despite the passage of seventy years, Miriam's ability to convey the constant shock, terror, and confusion that had permeated her early years, provides a unique perspective on the individual, very personal impact of the Nazis. That she was able at such a tender age, to maintain self-discipline, follow complex directions, and even help others, is a testimony to the spirit of Jewish resistance that was inherent in even the very young.

Here is Miriam's story . . .

Ann Arbor, Michigan, 2013

M y birth in beautiful, cosmopolitan Warsaw, Poland in 1935—the same year that Germany implemented its devastating anti-Semitic Nuremberg Laws—was joyously celebrated by both sides of our family. I was

Four-year-old Miriam
and her father,
Dr. Chaim Miasnik
Warsaw, Poland, 1939

named Miriam, but affectionately known as Mirele. As the only child of brilliant surgeon, Chaim Miasnik, and his lovely, elegant wife, Bronka, my future looked bright. Little did anyone know that soon, there would no longer be happy gatherings for our family. Or any Jewish family in Europe. The safety of my childhood home, which was filled with loving relatives, provided a stark contrast to the growing Nazi threats around us.

When relatives in the U.S. tried to convince my parents to leave Poland immediately, my maternal grandfather's response was that since millions of other European Jews weren't worried about Hitler, why should we be? So like so many others who couldn't foresee what was coming, we stayed. Similarly, like many other well-to-do Jews in the summer of 1939, our family went as usual to a lovely resort, where we played in the sun and ate the abundant, fresh, food—totally oblivious to the fact that our world had already ended without our knowledge. Soon after our return to Warsaw, however, it would seem as if our idyllic summer had been nothing more than a dream.

As soon as the war started, the Russians encouraged all able-bodied men to leave Warsaw and move to the Russian side of divided Poland. Since this region now included my father's hometown of Lida, he and my uncles decided to leave Warsaw. On September 1, 1939, when the Germans invaded Poland and began bombing its capital city of Warsaw, the events were beyond the comprehension of most adults. For a four-year-old child, it was like inhabiting a nightmare from which there was no awakening. I physically shook every time I heard the whistle of an incoming bomb, and before the shutters were tightly closed, I watched the fires outside in totally helpless bewilderment. The first time we went to a bomb shelter, my mother quickly packed food, water, and blankets, telling me not to panic, and that everything would be alright soon. We hurried down several flights of stairs and out to the street. There we were swept along with the terrified crowds, everyone dodging each other, as well as the bricks, glass, and burning debris that fell from exploding buildings. As we rushed to get into a bomb shelter, my mother told me in a voice I'd never heard before, to hang on to her at all times—that under no circumstances were we to separate from each other. "You must obey all the orders I give you without asking any questions. Do what I tell you, no matter what." Something about the strange, cold voice, and the bloodless expression on her face communicated the importance of following her directions.

We finally squeezed into a dark basement bomb shelter and found a corner where we could sit. Our refuge was strangely quiet as the people prayed that we would not be hit by a bomb. Whenever we heard the whistle of a bomb, everyone held their breath, until it passed us by. Suddenly, we heard the whistle and felt a bomb's impact. Our hearts seemed to stop beating as we waited to be torn to bits. But there was no explosion. Knowing that we would die at any moment, the terror in the room was almost electric. But nothing happened. Eventually, after the all-clear signal, a couple of the men dared to go upstairs to see what was what. Much to their surprise, they discovered that the bomb hadn't exploded because it had landed in a tub that was filled with water. The adults just shook their heads in wonder at this miracle. And we would think of it often during future bombardments.

After Warsaw fell, we decided to reunite in my father's hometown, Lida, which was then under Soviet occupation. So we packed what we could carry, and set off on a long, difficult journey, never imagining that it would be just the first of countless perilous journeys to come. My mother had tried to convince her parents to join us, but they'd felt it would be better for them to wait until we were settled and had a place for them to live. My paternal grandmother, who had come from her home in Lida to visit us for the summer, also decided for some reason, to stay in Warsaw. Torn as we were to leave them, we never dreamed that we'd never see them again.

In Lida, we were welcomed by my father and his brothers. The men had been able to find jobs, so we weren't as poor as most of the other Jews living under communism. What wasn't so much fun, however, was trying to find playmates. Even at that young age, the other little girls were conscious that I was different. They made fun of me because I didn't speak Yiddish, and my fancy city clothes were conspicuously out of place. I learned Yiddish quickly and told my mother I didn't want to wear my pretty clothes anymore. Once I looked and sounded like the other children, I was accepted by the group. It's interesting how even children will label and shun someone they view as an "outsider." How easy it is to fear and be cruel to someone who is different. And in the case of the Germans, how easy it was to decide that those who were seen as being "different," weren't even human beings, and therefore should be eliminated.

While I'm sure life under the Soviets was difficult for others, my parents were quite comfortable. I even began to feel safe again, as my memories of

Warsaw's horror were pushed to the back of my mind. In the summer of 1941, however, when I was six, this fragile sense of security was shattered when the Germans attacked the Soviet Union. Lida was one of their early targets. Once again, we heard the roaring of low-flying bomber planes, and the hideous whistling that preceded explosions and death all around us. Once again, my mother's face and voice changed, as she ordered me to obey her instantly—and at all times. She held me close for a moment and said that we needed to leave the house immediately. We packed some food and clothes and ran outside, past flaming houses, and on to the edge of town. I was terrified of becoming separated from my mother and being left on my own. When we finally found a place to stop and rest, we fearfully looked back and saw Lida in flames. My mother assured me that Papa and our other relatives were safe, and that we'd see them soon. I was still young enough to believe my mother, so in the midst of the chaos, I felt comforted.

When it seemed as if the fires had died down, we carefully picked our way through the smoldering wreckage back to town, apprehensive about what we'd see when we got to our street. Miraculously, our house was still standing. And my anxious father and relatives, who were waiting inside, were greatly relieved to see that we were safe. This safety, however, would not last. The Germans soon bombed Lida again, leaving even more devastation. Then, on Friday, June 27, 1941, German ground troops entered the city, and their goal was to kill the Jews of Lida. This time we could not escape. There was nowhere left to go. And as a child of six, with so many questions that no one was able to answer, I learned to keep my curiosity to myself, and stopped asking.

Soon, all Jews were ordered to sew yellow Stars of David to the front and back of their clothing, making us easy targets for abuse. Then, Jewish professionals, including my father, were ordered to come forward and identify themselves. Most of them were soon murdered. Since Papa was a surgeon, the Germans spared him because he was "useful." A week later, a *Judenrat*, as well as a Jewish police force were established to make sure that German commands were followed. Jewish men between ages fifteen and sixty were registered and sent on brutal slave-labor assignments outside of town. Sometimes these workers did not return. Women between the ages of sixteen and forty were also forced into hard labor. Constant hunger became normal. We had it a little better than the others because my father's job included performing surgery on Germans. This was exceedingly difficult for him, especially since his success rate would determine whether he—and his wife and daughter—would be allowed to live.

At the end of November 1941, the situation for Lida's Jews became even more desperate. Allowed to take only what they could carry, thousands were forced to abandon their homes, and then herded like cattle into what had now become a guarded ghetto. The soldiers seemed to have made a game out of shouting obscenities at the Jews, pushing them around, and humiliating and laughing at them as they trudged with their burdens toward their mystifying, terrifying, future. Eventually, we arrived at our "new home." It was a very small, dilapidated house, consisting of only four tiny rooms, and contained only the few pieces of furniture that hadn't been worth stealing. Each room housed at least two families, and if there was a bed, several people shared it. We were fortunate that before they'd been forcibly removed, the previous tenants had planted vegetables behind the house, so we did have some food. As the days passed, we tried to settle into a daily routine, and I even played with the other children in the ghetto.

In March 1942, when I turned seven, instead of the birthday celebration that most seven-year-olds might have expected, there occurred a major catastrophe. Almost seven hundred Jews, who were fleeing German atrocities in the Vilna Ghetto, had come to Lida. The Jews who were already living in the ghetto worked hard to find places for them to stay, and food for them to eat. Tragically for all of us, however, among these new refugees, there was also a criminal. One day he broke into and robbed the home of a beloved and respected priest, who had often risked his life to help the Jews. During the robbery, the burglar had also attacked and injured the priest, before escaping back to Vilna. The Germans responded by rounding up Lida's Jews, identifying and executing those from Vilna. This additional layer of unspeakable horror further heightened the terror that pervaded the ghetto. And not wanting to call attention to myself, or give my parents even more to worry about, I became quite adept at hiding my emotions, and kept my questions to myself.

Amidst the misery, a group of resourceful Jews came up with a good idea for making themselves "useful" to the Germans. They requested and were granted permission to set up numerous small workshops in a nearby technical school in order to manufacture items that the Germans needed. Although this arrangement, which showed productive Jewish workers, provided helpful propaganda photo opportunities for the Germans, there were also some positive results for Lida's Jews. One was that the craftsmen and artisans who made and repaired shoes, electrical supplies, clothing, paintings, toys, bags, and other goods, were given a little more food at lunch time. Another benefit of being considered "useful," was that it gave the factory workers the opportunity to set up a useful communication network amongst themselves. This was an example of how Jewish slave-laborers were still were able to devise a way to survive—as well as resist the Nazis—at least for a while.

On May 7, 1942, the ghetto was completely sealed and surrounded by police and their collaborators. What would become known as the great Jewish Massacre of Lida started early the next day. Even though it was May, the weather was very cold, and there was still snow on the ground. We were awakened by the Germans shouting for us all to come out and assemble on the street. Most people weren't even dressed yet. My mother grabbed my coat, shoes, and socks and we ran outside. I hung onto my parents' hands with all my strength. Then we were all ordered to line up and start marching out of town. Anyone who couldn't keep up was shot on the spot. We all were silent, knowing that we would be killed at the end of this march. The only sounds we heard were the shouting Germans, their barking dogs, and gunshots.

Suddenly, the line stopped, and we could hear the distinct sounds of multiple machine guns firing nonstop. German officials looked over all of our papers, and directed some people to go to the left, and the rest of us to go the right. We realized that being sent to the right, toward the sound of the machine guns, meant death. The soldiers beat us from behind with the butts of their guns to force us to run faster. Everyone was covered with blood. My parents held each of my hands tightly as we ran closer and closer to the machine gun fire. At this point, since there was no doubt that our lives were over, our only hope was that the end would be quick.

Then, much to our shock and disbelief, we heard a German yelling at us to go the other way. He grabbed my father and pushed him toward the people who'd been selected to live. He had recognized that my father was a surgeon, and would be needed by the Germans. And for reasons of his own, he allowed my mother and me to go with my father, thereby saving our lives. We stood until dusk along with the few others who had been spared. Then we all walked slowly back to the now almost deserted ghetto. During the next few days, however, Jews, from other towns were transported into the ghetto, so once again, it became overcrowded. And once again, craftsmen and artisans worked in the factory.

Since both of my parents were working, I spent most of my time alone. I was terrified that either they wouldn't come home, or that all the children would be murdered while their parents were working. Then at the beginning of the summer, 1942, a rumor began circulating that this is exactly what was going to happen. Once again, my mother's face and voice took on the cold tone that I knew meant something terrible was about to happen. She told me that the Germans actually were coming soon to kill the Jewish children. My parents, however, had a plan for me. I was going to have to pretend to be very sick. That way, my father could get me into the hospital. The very next day, Papa took me into a hospital ward and put me into a bed. Then he injected me with something that made me feel terribly sick and very tired. As long as I was sleeping, I wouldn't have to answer anyone's questions. He told me that even when I was awake, I should keep my eyes closed and pretend to sleep. Looking back, I can see that for a seven-year-old, this pretense was a very challenging act of anti-German resistance—although at the time, I was just following my father's orders.

This ploy kept me safe for a few days until my parents could make arrangements for me to go stay on a farm with a kind Gentile woman. My father had saved her little daughter from death, so she wanted to do the same for him. Of course this plan aroused all of my abandonment terrors, but I didn't have much time to worry, because my parents quickly took me out the side door of the hospital. A Gentile man that I didn't know was waiting for me in a shadowed cluster of trees. After handing me a small bag of clothing, my parents gave me final instructions that I still remember. "Listen and be quiet. Never speak Yiddish. From this day on, you are no longer a Jew. Pretend that you are an orphan and the farm woman's niece. Play with her little girl and help do chores. God willing, we will reunite in the future." Then they hugged me, turned, and walked away.

The stranger held my hand tightly, and led me in the opposite direction. Much as I wanted to wrench free and run back to my parents, I had been trained to follow their orders. So I held back my tears and forced myself to be brave, while wondering if I would ever see my parents again. During the several hours that we walked, the man tried to talk with me, but I was too frightened, confused, and angry at being abandoned to speak. Of course I couldn't have imagined that he was risking his life to save me. When we finally arrived at the farmhouse, the woman welcomed me warmly. She had told her four-year-old daughter that I was a cousin who would be staying with them for a while. The daughter was excited to have a new playmate who also watched out for her. I had no way of knowing that even this little Gentile girl now had to be careful about what she said to neighbors. She and her mother could be executed for taking me in.

I was overjoyed to see an actual bed, with clean sheets, soft pillows, and warm blankets that were just for me. Exhausted, I climbed in and immediately fell asleep. Awakened the next morning by the roosters, I got my bearings and started to cry when realized where I was. But since I knew that I had to be brave, I washed my face and put on a cheerful expression. It helped that I was given a wonderful breakfast, and told that I could eat as much as I wanted. As the days passed, I helped the woman and played with her daughter. At the same time, I was always on guard whenever anyone outside their family came by. I knew that they might recognize me as a Jew.

Sometimes I went to their church, where I learned how to kneel and cross myself, and look like I was praying. I understood that in order to avoid suspicion, I had to fit in. I couldn't look as if I were nervous or sad, or trying to avoid attention. After several weeks, it became apparent that the killing of ghetto children was not going to happen. One day, the man who had brought me to the farm returned, and took me back to my parents. I never saw him, the farm woman, or her daughter again, and I've often wondered if they survived. Their kindness to me put their lives in terrible danger, and there are no words to adequately express my family's gratitude to them.

After the Lida Massacre, the remaining Jews understood that they were not going to survive. Having no tradition of arming themselves and fighting, most had no idea how to defend themselves. Adding to their compliance, was the certainty of the German reprisals that would be unleashed at the slightest hint of resistance. In spite of this, however, a group of around one hundred and twenty young Jews decided that since they were going to die anyway, they might as well die fighting. And they wanted revenge. They managed to barter for, buy, or steal weapons from outside the ghetto. The group succeeded in assembling a collection of 33 rifles, as well as ammunition, grenades and other weapons. Their courageous leader, Baruch Levin, also manufactured weapons in his attic workshop. He used his mechanical skills to reassemble broken firearms, or transform them into other weapons, such as axes and knives.

It's important to understand that these resistance efforts were not universally supported by the other Jews in the ghetto. Those who worked in the German factories believed that they were safe, and could survive until the Allies liberated them. They thought the resisters would jeopardize the survival of the ghetto. This created great tension and hostility, sometimes within families. The resisters soon realized that they would have to leave the ghetto. They decided to join the Soviet partisans in the forest. Since my mother worked in the German factory, she had heard all about this, and brought the subject up with my father. They were frustrated because even if they tried to join the partisans, they'd be rejected because women and children were not wanted, and also because we didn't have any weapons to contribute. Soon, however, the partisans would give my parents no choice.

On Nov 9, 1942, the partisans in the Lipiczany Forest decided to bring a doctor back to their camp. They chose my father, because of his surgical skills. They also came for Baruch Levin, because of his mechanical skills and hoard of weapons. My mother told me that some men were coming to rescue us, and we would be leaving the ghetto that night. Again with the cold voice, she told me to act normally with my playmates so that no one would be suspicious. While I couldn't comprehend the idea of living in a forest, I felt relief to be leaving the horrors of the ghetto. And I was happy that my parents and I would be together. Later, I became afraid when I overheard the two partisans ask my father how it would be possible to take such a young child. They were afraid that I might cry out or make a disturbance that would give away their location. My father responded with confidence, "She is trained to follow orders. She has excellent self-discipline, and will be no problem." Apparently, the partisans believed him—or else they needed him so badly that they agreed to his condition that they also take my mother and me. Around midnight, they accompanied us as we silently crept out of the house, terrified that we'd be spotted and executed. When we arrived at a specific place at the barbed wire fence, the men used sharp clippers to make a small opening through which we could squeeze. Then they carefully rewired the fence so it wouldn't be obvious.

We continued along a small river. When we suddenly heard gunshots, we were terrified that we'd been spotted. The partisans motioned us to wade into the Lideika River and lower our bodies from view. Our hearts fluttering, we waited until the shooting stopped, and then we crossed to the other side of the river. Wet and cold, we continued walking until the men stopped and began digging. This seemed very mysterious to me. Was someone going to be killed and buried? Eventually, from the snow-covered earth, they uncovered some large bundles containing machine guns and ammunition that had been buried by the retreating Soviet army.

Now heavily armed and feeling more confident, our little group continued for several more hours. Just as the sun was rising, we arrived at a farm which the partisans indicated was safe for us to enter. They explained that the owner was a good communist who helped the partisans. Relieved to be safe and warm, we took off our wet clothes, hung them to dry, and collapsed for a few hours of sleep. When we awoke, the owner's wife fed us an amazing breakfast of freshly-baked bread and white farmer cheese. She even gave us hot Russian tea. These delicacies melted in our mouths, and warmed our hearts. Well-fed and dressed in dry clothes, we resumed our journey into the forest. Soon, the forest became so dense, and the fog became so heavy, that the sunlight couldn't break through. It seemed as if it had suddenly become night. Making our trek even more difficult was the layer of snow that hid any footpaths. Late that night, we finally reached the partisans' camp. We were tired, we were cold. And we were free.

The partisans congratulated us on our successful escape, sat us near a fire, and fed us a delicious hot meal of meat and potatoes. There were men and women in the camp, and hearing all the voices speaking Yiddish, I realized that I was in a group of Jews. How exciting it was to see strong, uncaged, courageous, competent Jews who weren't afraid to fight for themselves and their people! And they were all living in the forest! Our new home would be a *ziemlyanka*, a small, completely underground shed, with a small, well-hidden entrance. The top was covered with dirt, branches, and ground cover or snow, so there was no indication of what was below the surface. The interior was lined with logs for insulation, and included a raised wooden platform for sleeping. This tiny hideaway was a perfect size for me, but there wasn't even enough space for my parents to stand up straight.

Except for being in the middle of the forest, and filled with armed partisans, the camp was like a regular community. When I asked one of the guards if he was afraid, he laughed told me that he was not afraid, and that he was strong and "proud to be a Jewish fighter." This made me feel proud as well. While we did have warm clothing, since our shoes and boots wore out quickly from our constant trudging through the snowy forest, our feet were in danger of frostbite. Mama and I were assigned specific chores such as collecting wood and brush for fires, and we melted and stored snow for drinking and washing. Mama also helped cook, and I helped her as much as possible. At night, she and I would cuddle up to stay warm as we slept. Papa was usually away treating wounded partisans in scattered parts of our forest.

The partisans were like a military unit and their missions included raiding German troop encampments, bridges, roads, factories, trains, and train tracks. At night, in order to obtain food and other supplies, the partisans also attacked local farmers who were known to collaborate with the Germans. Farmers who helped the partisans were not attacked. A few weeks after we joined the partisans, we learned that Germans were on the way to capture and kill partisans and Jews in retaliation for recent partisan attacks. Our group had to quickly leave the camp for a safer location. Unfortunately, Mama and I were unable to keep up with them and we soon found ourselves with a small, barely-armed group of stragglers. We also soon became lost in the dense forest, without food or water.

One night, after many days of aimless wandering, our group found an unusual place to sleep. It was a deep pit that was hidden under the low branches of a massive spruce tree. Laying close together for warmth, we slept for a short time, when we were jolted awake by the sound of German voices. Trembling with fear, we seemed to stop breathing until they passed by—only a few yards away from us. If it had been daylight, they would have seen our footprints in the snow. After a fitful sleep, we set off again, hoping to find some partisans that would take us. Mama and I eventually became separated from our group, and terror-stricken, freezing, and starving, we tried to keep each other's hopes up.

After what was probably two weeks, we saw a partisan scout, and told him who we were. Much to our relief, he informed us that Papa was alive and well, and took us to him. It was a joyous reunion, one I shall never forget. Papa was amazed and proud that we had survived alone in the vast and cold wilderness, and so were we. He took us to a Jewish family camp located nearby, where we had our first hot meal in weeks. That night as we lay side by side near a small burning fire, I felt safe again. During our few weeks at the family camp, one of our biggest challenges was the ever-present lice that roamed freely over our bodies, biting as they moved from one person to the next. Since lice transmit many infectious diseases, including the deadly typhus, we did everything we could to get rid of them. Standing half-naked in the snow, we would squash them one at a time between our fingernails. This needed to be done repeatedly. Another problem was the lack of food. We just lived one day at a time, never knowing when or if we would eat again, and in constant fear of Germans and their collaborators.

We soon learned that our camp was about to be raided. Leaving quickly, we were careful to drag branches in the snow behind us to hide our footprints. We camped for a few days in an area that was dense with tall trees, which Papa and I climbed in order to spot any incoming danger. Lacking food, and unable to light a fire, we were hungry and cold. We finally received word from a passing partisan scout that all was clear, and we returned to the family camp. My father was usually away treating patients under the worst possible conditions, in remote sections of the forest. He had little equipment, no staff, no anesthesia, antibiotics, or a sterile operating room. Since he had so many patients, Papa had to keep moving, and was unable to provide follow-up care. Eventually, my father was able to convince the Soviet commander that a hospital needed to be built in the forest. As outlandish as this might seem, under my father's leadership, it was accomplished!

First they had to find a good location. They scouted around and finally decided on a small, remote island that was completely surrounded by vast swamps. They felt that the site would be difficult for Germans to find and capture. Their next challenge was to create a way to actually get on the island. There was no way to build a bridge, so they came up with the idea of using floating logs. The partisans would step unsteadily from log to log, while carrying patients on their backs or on stretchers. Sometimes, the carriers slipped and fell into the swamp, and great effort was required to fish them all out. Large *ziemlyankas* were dug to provide housing for the patients and the staff. Another was set up as the operating and recovery room. A separate facility was built for partisans who were ill with infectious diseases. Partisans raided local hospitals for supplies, including surgical instruments, medications, anesthetics, and even some hospital beds, electric generators, and lights.

My father was able to staff the hospital with two Jewish doctors and several nurses who had escaped from various ghettos, bringing desperately needed supplies and equipment with them. Women from nearby camps took care of the housekeeping. Soon, Mama and I were able to move to the island. We lived in a *ziemlyanka* with thirty staff members. By this point, I had adapted to the forest, and grown comfortable in the wilderness. For my personal safety, and to protect me from rape, Papa had shaved off my hair, and I dressed in boys' clothing. I felt safer and more powerful pretending I was a boy. Everyone agreed that I looked like a real partisan. Many of the partisans had lost their own families, and so as the only child, I was treated with warmth and great kindness.

My most extraordinary experiences were being able to watch my father's surgeries. There were hundreds of them, and I was determined not to miss any—even those that took place late at night. His patients were riddled with bullet wounds, and in the absence of anesthetics, frequently writhing in pain. Sometimes they had to be knocked unconscious. I saw stomachs being cut open and intestines exposed. Papa would cut out the damaged areas, and then reconnect the clean-cut ends. Chest cavities were cut open with a saw and dead pieces of lung removed—some still containing bullets. I watched as feet and arms were amputated with saws. Miraculously, most of the partisans who had been operated on survived their surgeries. Those who did die usually succumbed to infections. Amidst the dangers, the terror, and injuries, however, there were moments of peace and beauty. On the occasional quiet evenings, we lit campfires and sang Yiddish, Polish and Russian songs, and even some opera arias. My father sang Zionist and Hebrew songs of Palestine.

In addition to dressing like a boy, I was determined to be as strong and productive as a boy. I gathered wood for fires, and carried large logs for building new structures. I helped the nurses sterilize materials for surgeries. I sometimes helped the posted guards on the other side of the swamp, camouflaged trails, and scouted out the surrounding areas for safety. I developed an eye for detail and real talent for finding my way in the forest. I kept track of specific features, such as bark colors of specific trees, unusually spaced bushes, and formations of trees. One day, when I had accompanied my mother on her sentry-duty assignment, we were approached by partisans who were coming back into the camp. The rule was that no one would be allowed in without stating the frequently changing password. Mama pointed her rifle at them, and demanded the password. When they didn't reply, I ran to tell Papa. He came back with me and spoke to the men. At first they were angry, but when they realized that it was Dr. Miasnik's wife who had pointed her gun at them, they apologized. They even commended her for being such a good guard.

On my eighth birthday, I received a very special gift. My father presented it to me saying, "Mirele, you are now old enough to have a gun of your own." Beaming with pleasure and surprise, I thanked my parents, telling them that it was the best gift I could ever receive. The pistol, which was small and dainty, had been confiscated by a partisan from a captured German officer, who had apparently planned to give it to his girlfriend as a present. In my boyish military uniform, and with the pistol proudly worn in a special holster on my side, I felt like a real partisan. It made me feel safe, and I wore it all the time. Eventually, after I was trained in how to use the gun, I was given bullets. I already knew how to take care of it because being skilled with my hands, I had often cleaned the partisans' machine guns and rifles. I would take them apart screw by screw, clean them, and then reassemble them.

I soon learned the hard way how dangerous it would be for a partisan to lose a weapon. I had gone off to the bushes to the "bathroom," which was just a hole, and I had hung my holstered gun on a nearby branch. When I was through, I carelessly forgot to retrieve the gun, and left it hanging. Not long afterwards, when our Russian commander went to the same place for the same reason, of course he found the gun and he decided not to tell me. I was terribly upset with myself for what I considered a grave failure. Finally, the chief must have decided that I'd learned my lesson. He walked up to me and somehow managed to keep from laughing as he handed it back to me, and sternly warned me that, "It is a crime for a partisan to lose a gun." Needless to say, I did not lose the gun again, and only gave it up upon our liberation. A few weeks later, we'd heard that the Germans were coming our way, so we ran to hide in a swampy marsh. We stood perfectly still, with our own guns pointed at our foreheads. We were not going to be captured alive. Better to shoot ourselves with dignity, and die by our own hands. Fortunately, the Germans gave up on finding us and left. Again, we all returned to the hospital.

By the late winter of 1944, I had been with the partisans for more than a year, and survived many more German attacks. Now, we began to hear through our radio receivers rumors that the Germans were finally being beaten back by the Soviets. In June 1944, the Russian army was fast approaching. While this was good news, it ironically also brought new dangers, because the defeated and fleeing Germans came to the forest to hide from the Soviets. So what had once been a haven for Jews, was now becoming a haven for the Germans. Fortunately, this would soon end with liberation. When the Soviet army finally came, partisans from near and far converged to meet our liberators. We greeted the Russian soldiers ecstatically. With tears in our eyes, we welcomed our heroic liberators with flowers, hugs, and kisses. Together with my father and the others, I saluted the soldiers, and when I kissed one, he complimented my father on his brave "son." Along with the joy, however, the Soviets also brought unexpected misery. They forcibly recruited many partisans to fight at the battle front, which was then in northeast Poland. The lives of many partisans who had survived ghettos, forced labor, and living and fighting in the forests, ended tragically, as they fought and died for the Soviets.

During the months immediately after liberation, we viewed the Russians as our saviors. I proudly wore a red scarf around my neck, and sang the many patriotic Russian songs that I'd learned from the partisans. I even joined the *Komsomol*, a communist youth group. The Soviets considered my father to be a hero, and awarded him the prestigious *Order of Lenin*. They appointed him the chief of staff at their hospital in Szczuczyn, Belarus, and provided us with a nice house to live in. Always excited about learning, and eager to go to school, I was enrolled in the third grade, even though I'd had no previous schooling. Fortunately, none of the other children had been to school either, so I didn't feel out of place. While it was exciting and fun to finally be able to associate with other children, my body's immune system, which hadn't been exposed to childhood diseases, wasn't up to the sudden onslaught of my young friends' germs. I became seriously ill, first with whooping cough, which necessitated my being quarantined, then, with mononucleosis, and shortly thereafter, pneumonia. I languished in bed for months, becoming weaker and sicker. I thought that I'd never stop coughing. I was completely isolated and bedridden until the end of the year.

It soon became apparent that the reality of communism bore no resemblance to its alleged ideals. The system was corrupt, and allowed little if any personal freedom. Food was scarce, and the basic necessities for daily life were almost non-existent. Anti-Semitism was rampant—it was as if many of the

Gentiles resented Jews for surviving. Strict travel restrictions were imposed, especially on professionals such as physicians, who were considered "essential" to the good of the community. The Soviets were afraid, with good reason, that these professionals would leave as soon as possible. Our family could not continue to live under the extreme restrictions and dangers of communism. We realized that we had to go where we could be free. Since we had relatives in America, that is where my parents decided we would go. This decision was the beginning of yet another long and perilous journey.

As had often happened in the past, people who Papa had saved, helped us. One of these was a colonel in the Soviet air force, whose life Papa had saved through an emergency operation. My father confided to him that we wanted to go to Poland with his unit. The grateful colonel and his brigade were about to leave for Poland, and at great risk to himself, he offered to take us with them on their military train. Once again, we had to sneak away, with only what we could carry. As we feared, the Russian secret police soon found out about our escape, and started looking for us. Fortunately for us, they never suspected we'd be on a military train, so they only looked for us on all departing *civilian* trains. We later heard that in order to explain our abrupt disappearance, as well as the intense Soviet hunt for us, that Papa had been officially accused of robbing the municipal hospital. If the NKVD (the Soviet secret police organization later known as the KGB) had found us, we would have been sent to die in some Siberian prison camp.

Aboard the train, the Russian soldiers were very warm and welcoming—especially because we'd been partisans. Together, we sang Russian patriotic songs and exchanged life stories. They recounted battles they'd fought, and comrades who had been lost. Fortunately, the trip was uneventful, and two days later we arrived in Bialystok, in northern Poland. After saying goodbye to the soldiers and wishing them well, we boarded a civilian train and headed south for the city of Lublin in central Poland, where my parents hoped to live until further plans could be made for our future. When we arrived, because there was a severe housing shortage, my mother made arrangements for us to share an apartment building with a group of Jewish families in circumstances similar to ours. There was very little furniture, but we felt safe and happy to be in our own apartment. We were especially happy to be able to celebrate our first Passover in six years. Along with this happiness, however, came great pain at the absence of our beloved relatives who had been murdered.

All too soon, we were confronted again with vicious anti-Semitism. One morning on the way to buy some food, my father was cornered by young ruffians who threw rocks at him while screaming anti-Jewish obscenities. They demanded to know why he hadn't been killed. Papa managed to get home safely, but my mother, who looked Gentile, did the food shopping from then on. She also decided to go to Warsaw to see what had become of our family and our home. She was devastated to see the once beautiful city in ruins, and to learn that all of our relatives had been murdered. There was nothing left.

My parents realized that we had to get out of Poland as soon as possible. As refugees, we needed identification papers for further travel. Fortunately, an underground Jewish group that assisted Holocaust survivors had provided us with false documents. Papa met a Soviet soldier who was driving a truck to Czechoslovakia, and who, for a small payment, agreed to take us along. That night, we once again quietly left our apartment while the others slept, and walked to where the truck picked us up. We drove through Czechoslovakia, and soon arrived in Soviet-occupied Hungary. Next, we took a train to Hungary's border with Romania, at which point, along with a small group of refugees, got off the train and were smuggled across the border. Then, we had to climb the Carpathian Mountains. All of this physical exertion intensified my cough, and I could barely breathe. Eventually, we arrived at Turda, a small city in the mountains, where some fifty other Jewish refugees had established a *kibbutz*. They welcomed us and assigned us to a small room for sleeping, but the kitchen, laundry, eating areas, as well as other public rooms, were shared by all. Eventually my parents, who valued their privacy, were able to rent a room for us in town.

Turda was very interesting to me because the Jewish community that had been there for generations had not been subjected to German persecution, so they had remained safe and even prosperous. These Jews were very kind, and provided us with money and clothing. We were able to rest there for a few weeks until we were unexpectedly confronted by two challenges. First, my father had to have surgery for a very painful hernia, and second, while he was still recuperating, the Soviet army invaded Romania. The leaders of the *kibbutz* warned us to leave Turda while we still had the chance. It seemed that no matter how far we traveled, we still could not get away from the communists. And so, on a hot, summer day, with Papa barely able to travel, we boarded the first train out—which was headed back to Budapest. The train soon became overwhelmingly crowded as it picked up groups of peasants, carrying small farm animals. The animals' stench fouled the air, and made everyone nauseous. Just when it looked as if no one, and nothing else, could squeeze on board, a newly arrived group of armed Russian soldiers evicted us all from the train, so that they could transport their own soldiers to Hungary. Angered by this latest misery, the other passengers, along with their animals started to get rowdy, and climbed up on the roofs of the train cars. As soon as we managed to join them, the Russians chased us off. They had decided to let some civilians ride in two of the cars. There was utter chaos as the crowds tried to squeeze into those two cars. Those who didn't make it, made their way back up to the roofs. Somehow, we were fortunate, and made it inside.

Because of the unbearable heat and the overcrowded space, many people began to faint. Papa, who was still weak from his surgery, decided he'd had enough, so he got off the train and walked up to a group of Soviet officers. In his best Russian, introduced himself saying, "*Tavarishch* (friend), I am Dr. Miasnik. I fought the Germans as a partisan in Belorussia." The officers who were impressed with Papa's flawless Russian and his heroic service during the war, welcomed him to one of their comfortable cars. When he told them about his wife and daughter, the officers said that we were also welcome to join them. For the rest of the trip we were able to breathe clean air and eat wonderful food. My parents enjoyed sharing stories with the soldiers, but directed me to remain silent so that I wouldn't accidentally let anyone know that we were escaping from communism. When we arrived in Budapest, we were horrified to learn that the peasants who had stayed on the roofs of the train cars had all been sucked off by the vacuum created when the train, barreling along at full speed, went through the mountain tunnels. We were shaken as we realized how close we had come to a grisly death. Our lives had been saved by the Soviet soldiers.

Conditions in Budapest were terrible. We couldn't find a place to stay, so we ended up sleeping with other refugees on the floors of an apartment building. As soon as he could, Papa again found and paid a truck driver to take us out of Hungary. One afternoon, as our truck climbed the Alps, we came to a border-crossing in the middle of nowhere. Fortunately for us, the Russian guards there had been paid off by Jewish Relief organizations that were helping Jews to escape the Soviets. While we were relieved to have finally escaped the communists, we were impoverished, displaced persons, and no longer citizens of any country. My parents couldn't legally work or travel, and I couldn't go to school. We just moved from one small, makeshift DP camp to another, living from day to day, and never knowing what would happen next. And since we didn't have time to make friends, we were always strangers in a crowd.

One day, some tough looking, heavily armed soldiers came to our camp and announced that we were going to Italy. I didn't even know what or where Italy was. We were frightened by them, but having no choice, we obeyed their shouted commands to climb into the backs of their five trucks. A few miles later, our terror turned to astonishment, when they informed us that they were part of the British Army's Jewish Brigade! We hadn't known such a thing even existed. They spoke reassuringly to us in Yiddish, telling us not to be afraid, and that we were safe with our Jewish protectors. Overwhelmed with relief and exhaustion, we settled down for our long ride in the truck. After driving through the Alps, our caravan arrived in a small military camp in northern Italy by morning. We learned that our rescuers were members of *Bricha*, an underground Jewish Relief organization that arranged escapes and border-crossings for Holocaust Jews. They were part of an extensive clandestine network whose mission was to get Jewish refugees into Palestine in violation of British Blockade. Clearly, strong Jewish resistance to oppression was active and effective even after the war had ended.

After a series of moves, we ended up renting a room in Venice for ten months, and Papa was able to earn a little money by taking care of refugees' medical needs. Then the Jewish relief agencies sent us to Rome, where we shared a villa with other Jewish refugees. Despite our many differences, we shared one common bond: we were all wandering Jews. New families kept arriving, and much to my delight, some brought children. We were especially happy when we were reunited with a few who we'd known from the partisans or from Romania. My parents quickly enrolled me in the fourth grade of a regular Italian school in Rome. Since I'd been brought up in the forests, had had no education, and couldn't yet read Italian, I struggled in school for about three months and was quite miserable.

Fortunately, in February 1947, with the help of my uncles in America, my parents were finally able to work through the oppressive bureaucratic complications of immigration, and we boarded a ship for America. Upon our arrival in New York, while I was surprised that the fabled "streets of gold" were actually littered with garbage, I was grateful to be in a free country. The process of becoming Americanized at my age was complicated by the beginnings of adolescence, and inability to speak English. Once again, I was placed in a school where I had no chance of succeeding, and I was labeled as lazy and unmotivated to learn. This couldn't have been further from the truth, but there wasn't anything I could do about it. I buried my frustration, and became isolated at a time when I hungered to be part of the group. Also deeply buried were my experiences in Europe. No one wanted to hear about the horror.

Determined to make up for my deficiencies, I quickly learned English, worked hard to make up for lost time, and managed to graduate high school at age seventeen. After graduating from New York University, I earned my Masters' Degree in bacteriology from the University of Michigan. I also met and fell in love with an amazing, and brilliant man, Henry Brysk, who had earned his PhD. in theoretical physics from Duke University on his 23rd birthday. Henry had fled from Vichy, France to Portugal with his family in 1941 when he was twelve, so we'd had many similar experiences. We married in June 1955. The first of our two precious daughters, Judith, who is now a physician, was born in 1957. Havi, who is an artist and therapist, was born in 1959. While the girls were still small, I returned to graduate school and received a PhD in Biological Sciences from Columbia University in December 1967. When we relocated to San Diego, I was a postdoctoral fellow at the University of California branch there. In the 1970s, I was awarded a Fellowship at the University of Michigan, and then another from the National Institute of Health, researching basal cell carcinoma. Next, I became a research assistant professor at the University of New Mexico, and in 1979, I was offered a tenure-track position at the University of Texas Medical Branch where I became an assistant professor of dermatology and was awarded joint appointments in the departments of microbiology and in biochemistry. In 1988, when I was promoted to full professor, I began the most creative journey I had ever traveled. For years I had only dreamed of being an independent scientist doing my own research, and now I was actually doing it—and publishing my results. I was even allowed to design a new spacious laboratory that was lauded for being most custom-built on campus—and the envy of many other scientists.

After a long, successful career as a scientist and in academia, I retired in

December, 1999. In the absence of my always hectic and demanding schedule, I soon began to experience occurrences of post-traumatic stress syndrome. A lifetime of pent-up horror was now manifesting itself in severe depression. Fortunately, I sought and received outstanding therapy, and over several years, was able to come to terms with my childhood experiences. Instead of expending intense energy keeping everything buried, I began to allow the past to come to the surface, and to integrate it with my current reality. This process of expressing my emotions was facilitated through my long-postponed interest in art.

My first venture into art was through stark black-and-white photography in which I sought to express human emotions through the facial expressions and body language of my subject. My acrylic paintings in the 1980s depicted the raw pain of my childhood experiences, as I was reliving them through psychotherapy. As my soul was healing, by conveying life's flow, celebration, and continuity through my art, I was finally able to experience joy in spite of the shadows. In the late 1990s, the computer became my most important tool, and the computer monitor became my canvas. In 2002, bolstered by the success of my therapy, and inspired by my art, I felt that I was strong enough to return to Poland. I cried my way through the entire trip, as the gaping wounds of my past reopened, but I was finally able to let those memories come to the surface. I felt a deep need to portray the humiliation and suffering of Hitler's victims, thereby returning to them their dignity as human beings and as Jews.

When I returned home, I embarked upon a mission to recreate memory through art. I chose photographs of actual Jews who perished, including those of my own family. I use images of real victims individually, so as to personalize the Holocaust. While the Germans wanted to dehumanize the Jews, I want to reverse that process and remember each victim, one at a time, not just as the gigantic, collective number *six million*. I decided to show each person's face, and to tell that person's story within the context of history. Through my "art of remembrance," I finally was able to stop burying the pain that had for so long diminished the joy of my life. And I was eventually able to stop feeling guilty for surviving the Holocaust when so many others had perished. Instead, I have focused on living a life they would have wanted to live themselves—a life that includes both pain and glory—a life they would have been proud of.

Whenever I tell my story to students, or create an artwork, I become so immersed mentally and emotionally in the historic events, that I am surprised at the end to realize how much time has passed. How could it be 2014, when just moments ago, it was 1940? How is it that I now have grandchildren who are older than I was during the Holocaust? I am so very grateful for the opportunities I have had not only to live a rich and rewarding life, but to have been able contribute something of value through science and through art. Despite the heinous hardships of World War II, I have been able to realize my dreams, including some I never knew I had!

Although I had to relinquish my childhood, I was able to earn a PhD., and become a scientist, professor, and now, an artist. I was able to fall in love, and marry an extraordinary man, and we will soon celebrate our 59th anniversary. Our two beautiful and accomplished daughters have blessed us with five precious, loving grandchildren. I know that I share the feelings of other Holocaust survivors when I say that our descendants are our answer to Hitler's "Jewish Question." It is through them that we can be assured that the Jewish People will endure and thrive . . . and continue the Jewish legacy of Tikkun—healing the world.

In the aftermath of my return to Poland in 2002, I realized that I had yet another goal to accomplish: I needed to document the truth of the Holocaust so that others would know what really happened. And so I began to write my memoir, which I entitled, *Amidst the Shadows of Trees*. I was especially pleased when it was published in 2013 by Gihon River Press. I soon decided to use my art to teach about the Holocaust, and along with the extraordinary Margaret Lincoln, PhD., and a group of outstanding teachers, wrote a second book, *The Stones Weep*, which was also published in 2013 by Gihon River Press. Beginning in 2001, my artwork has been exhibited continuously in both solo and group shows. Details and reviews of my art and books can be found at http://miriambrysk.com/. I am honored and profoundly grateful that my work has received praise, thereby validating that my commitment to showing the truth of the Holocaust is of value. This is how I honor those who were lost. And as long as I can speak, write, and use a computer, I will never stop.

Miriam in front of a montage from her exhibit, *In a Confined Silence.*
Central to this piece, entitled, "Mama and I," is a 1944 photograph
of Miriam and her mother, Bronka. The images along the bottom
show her family before the war.

Epilogue

Unlike Manya, Faye, Lola and Miriam, most of the countless Jewish and Gentile females who defied the Nazis perished without their deeds ever being known. With few, if any, resources, and so little hope, why did these women, unlike so many others, choose to defy oppression? Despite their many differences, what qualities did they share that compelled them to fight? Did any survive? If so, what happened to them after the war? After talking with them, it became clear that whether rich or poor, rural or urban, these remarkable women did not see themselves as heroines. Instead, they each insist that they were just ordinary people who, when confronted with the senseless Nazi horror, just did the only thing that made any sense: they did the right thing. And seventy-plus years later, as their stories reveal, they have never stopped "doing the right thing."

Despite differences in age, education, and economic circumstances, there is much unity in their beliefs. The same ideas and phrases are repeated throughout their stories. They each experienced the incomprehensibility of what the Germans had brought to Poland. They each felt guilt that they survived when so many others did not. They each felt that somehow, they hadn't done enough. Religion played an important role in each of their lives. They each had been helped by Polish Gentiles. They each feel that their descendants are, and will continue to be, the Jewish answer to Hitler's Final Solution to the Jewish Question. They each have dedicated their lives to Holocaust education, and honoring the victims of the Germans.

The historically unprecedented and convulsive years during which Manya, Faye, Lola, and Miriam defied and transcended Nazi oppression, would leave Poland devastated politically, socially, and economically. They also left Poland devoid of its former ethnic minorities, primary among which were its Jews. In 1939, before World War II, there had been approximately 3.5 million Jews, ten percent of the total population, living in Poland. At the end of the war, in 1945, it has been estimated that fewer than 50,000 remained. Since so many Jews lacked identification papers, and many others were using false identities, it was impossible to make an accurate count. Most of them would leave Poland as soon as possible. The reason for their rapid post-war departure was that their families had been exterminated, their communities had been destroyed, and most of the few Jewish homes that had somehow survived, were now inhabited by Poles. Making matters worse was the fact that deadly anti-Semitism still existed in some areas of Poland. Furthermore, the post-World War II border changes, along with the Soviet communist takeover, confused government jurisdictions, preventing old records that would confirm Jewish property ownership and provide property and life insurance benefits, from being found.

Under communism, life for the people of Poland was very hard. They were isolated from the rest of the world, food and consumer products were in short supply, and basic human freedoms, including freedom of the press and religion, as well as freedom to travel, were restricted or eliminated. There was nothing left in Poland for the Jews. And there was very little left of Poland for the Poles, who would continue to live under communist oppression until 1989. During this time, there was no one to tell the truth about the role of Poland in the Holocaust. No book publishers were turning out books about Righteous Poles. There was no film industry making movies about resistance heroes. And although there were many firsthand accounts of brutal anti-Semitism, thousands accounts of Polish heroism on behalf of Jews, such as those of Zegota members, remained largely unknown. For decades, the German concentration and extermination camps in Poland were erroneously considered to be Polish camps.

Following the fall of communism in Poland, barriers to information and religious freedom were removed. This finally allowed Polish Gentiles to learn—and to tell the truth—about the Holocaust. There is, however, still a challenge to determine the number of Jews living in Poland today. This is because in addition to the frequently changing identities during the war, many Jewish-born adults in Poland today only survived the Holocaust because as young children, they'd been taken in by Gentile families. When no one came to claim these children, they were raised as Catholics, and therefore do not even know they are Jews. Ironically, some very religious Catholic Poles have recently discovered that they are really Jewish. And while there are those who are eager to find their relatives, and learn about Jewish life and history, there are others who prefer to keep their Jewish roots a secret. Today the total population of Poland is approximately thirty eight million. Estimates of the Jewish population vary widely, but there probably are only 5,000–20,000, with most residing in Warsaw and Krakow.

Along with freedom from communism, also came the freedom to be a Polish Jew. And much to the benefit of all Poles, there has also begun a lively resurgence of Jewish culture. For the first time, young Poles are learning the truth about the long and rich history of Jews in Poland. And what they are learning is that the history of Poland and the history of Jews are inextricably partnered. Rising from the ruins, are new state-of-the-art Jewish community centers, museums, libraries, and synagogues. Jewish holidays, rituals, weddings, *Bar* and *Bat Mitzvahs* are once again freely celebrated. Jewish schools are well-attended, and public schools, which are open to all, include Holocaust Education in their curricula. Jewish Studies Programs are popular in universities. Summer camps, bookstores, restaurants, festivals, theaters, newspapers, and even a popular Polish-Jewish monthly magazine, *Midrasz*, provide further evidence that the Jewish community is firmly planted and growing in Poland. Strong, healthy and committed partnerships, officially encouraged and financially supported by the Polish government, are forming between the Jewish and Polish communities. These partnerships provide powerful resources in battling any still-existing anti-Semitism, giving hope and confidence that the future of Poland will be a richly textured, and mutually beneficial partnership of Jews and Gentiles. How fortunate that Manya, Faye, Lola, and Miriam have lived to see Poland overcome its anti-Semitic past. How gratifying it must be for them to know that Polish Jews and Gentiles are now working together as partners to enrich the future of their shared homeland.

Appendices

Reader-Discussion Guide

Pre-Reading:

1. Describe a time when you had to decide between being a victim, bystander, perpetrator or resister. What did you do, and why did you do it? What was the outcome?

2. What do you already know about the lives of Jewish and Gentile women in Poland during the years between the end of World War I and the end of World War II?

3. In what ways do you think life for Jewish and Gentile Polish women during the 1920s–1940s were both similar and different?

Post-Reading:

1. How did the rise of Nazism affect the daily lives of Polish Jewish and Gentile women?

2. Compare and contrast the qualities and circumstances that characterized Gentile and Jewish Female Resistance to the German-occupation of Poland.

3. Compare and contrast the lives of Jewish and Gentile Polish women with those of Jewish and Gentile Polish men during the Third Reich.

4. What factors led Manya, Faye, Lola, and Miriam to resist the Nazis? What did they have in common? How did they differ?

5. How did the lives of Jewish and Gentile females before, during and after the war reflect their characters?

6. In what ways have your perspectives of Jewish and Gentile Polish females' response to the Nazis changed/not changed?

7. If you could travel back through time, what would your life be like as a Polish Jewish or Gentile female during the Holocaust? As a Polish Gentile female?

8. Describe how you and your family would respond if an enemy invaded and occupied your country today.

9. What are some ways society can address the issue of bullying in the schools?

10. In what ways can society address 21st century genocides?

Glossary

Active Resistance: taking physical action to defy oppression. Examples: joining a Partisan fighting group in the forest; hiding Jews from the Germans; delivering secret documents to resistance workers.

Aktions: deadly attacks against Jews that were carried out by Germans and their sympathizers, often in the middle of the night. They usually included the roundup and deportation of survivors to extermination camps.

The Allied Military Forces: in World War II, these consisted primarily of the United States, Britain, France, and the Soviet Union. Australia, Belgium, Brazil, Canada, China, Denmark, Greece, the Netherlands, New Zealand, Norway, Poland, South Africa, and Yugoslavia were also participants.

Anti-Semitism: the hatred of Jews for no reason other than their race, or ethnicity.

Armia Krajowa: the underground Polish Home Army, the military force that actively fought the Germans in World War II.

Aryan Master Race: Hitler's description of the tall, blonde, blue-eyed people who came from Northern (Nordic) regions, and who Hitler considered superior to all others, and therefore destined to rule all others.

Auschwitz: also known as Auschwitz-Birkenau, was the largest of the German concentration and death camps, and functioned from 1940 until 1945. Located near Krakow, in southern Poland, Auschwitz was first a detention center for political prisoners. However, it soon became the center of a network of several camps where Jews and other "enemies" of the Germans were either immediately exterminated (usually in gas chambers) or worked to death. Some prisoners were also victims of monstrous medical experiments. More than one million people were murdered at Auschwitz.

Austro-Hungarian Empire: a monarchy that existed from 1867 until the end of World War I in 1918. Today's countries of Austria, Hungary, Slovenia, Bosnia and Herzegovina, Croatia, the Czech Republic, and even parts of Italy, Poland, and Ukraine were once part of this Empire.

Axis Military Powers: in World War II, these partners were Germany, Italy, Japan, Hungary, Romania, and Bulgaria.

Blitzkreig: the German word for "lightning war." This was the their method of attacking Poland on September 1, 1939.

British Blockade of Palestine: at the end of World War II, Palestine was still under the administration of the British Mandate, which had been created by the League of Nations in 1923. It gave the British administrative control over some regions that had been part the Ottoman Empire until the end of World War I. In 1939, in response to the influx of Jews to Palestine as a result of Europe's anti-Semitism, the British felt it was necessary to limit the number of Jewish refugees allowed into Palestine. This "Blockade" led to violence, death, and the incarceration of over 50,000 Jewish refugees in internment camps on the island of Cyprus from 1946–1952. In 1939 a secret Jewish organization, called Aliya Bet, was established in order to smuggle Jews into Palestine, despite fierce military opposition from Britain and the USSR. The United Nations ended the British Mandate, and thus the Blockade, in 1947.

Central Powers: World War I (1914–18) partnership of Germany, the Austro-Hungarian Empire, and the Ottoman Empire, that fought against the Allies, or Entente Powers: France, Great Britain, Russia, Italy, and eventually, the United States.

Chancellor: the leader of Germany's government.

Collective Guilt: the concept that held all family members—and sometimes even entire villages—responsible for any Pole who might have helped Jews, and therefore subject to execution.

Communism: a form of government where all property is publicly owned and people work and are paid according to their abilities and needs. In 1917, following the Russian Revolution when Communists took over the government, Russia became officially known as the Union of Soviet Socialist Republics (USSR). In Soviet Communism, the dictatorial government planned and controlled the economy, claiming that its goal was to equalize the social classes. In practice, it created many tragic hardships for the people, and was finally dissolved in 1991, leaving Russia once again its own country.

Concentration Camps: brutal, usually deadly, prison camps, established in Germany in 1933 to incarcerate and punish anyone thought to be a threat to the Nazis. Concentration camps were previously used by the British in its Boer Wars (1899–1902) against the South African Republic and the Republic of the Orange Free State.

Crusades (1095–1798): a series of wide-ranging and murderous religious conflicts, known as "Holy Wars," authorized by the Roman Catholic Church, and involving several hundred thousand Christian Crusaders (Knights). The purpose of the First Crusade was to journey from Europe to the Holy Land in order to restore Christianity there. Subsequent Crusades would take them throughout Europe and the Middle East. Wherever they went, the Crusaders inflicted massive destruction and death upon "infidels" or "non-believers" along the way. Their victims included hundreds of thousands of Jews—thus providing a grisly prototype for later pogroms.

Einsatzkommandos: mobilized German killing-squads that were sent in advance of invading German troops in order to kill Polish and Jewish intellectuals and other leaders, thereby ensuring that the general population would be easier to control.

Entente Powers: allies in World War I, included the French Republic, the British Empire, the Russian Empire, and eventually, Italy. Japan, Belgium, Serbia, Greece, Montenegro, Romania, and Czechoslovakia were also partners with the Allies.

Extermination Camps: established in Poland by the Germans as efficient killing centers. The first opened at Chelmno in 1941, and used mobile gas vans to kill Jews and other "undesirables." In 1942, killing centers at Belzec, Sobibor, Treblinka and Auschwitz systematically murdered the Jews of the General Gouvernement. The Germans soon constructed huge gas chambers to increase killing efficiency.

Final Solution to the Jewish Question: Hitler's campaign to exterminate the Jewish People. It later became known as the Holocaust, or the Shoah.

Genocide: (*genos* from the Greek for "people," and *cidium* from the Latin for "killing") is the deliberate and organized obliteration of an entire race or ethnic group of people. Hitler's Final Solution was a campaign of genocide against the Jews.

Gentiles: people who are not Jewish.

German Empire (1871–1918): also known as the German *Reich* (Realm), was a great industrial power ruled by Emperor Wilhelm I. After World War I, and Wilhelm's abdication, the Empire ceased to exist, and Germany became the democratic Weimar Republic.

German General Gouvernement: the separate administrative region of the Third Reich that included much of central and southern Poland, Warsaw, Kraków, and Lviv, as well as western Ukraine, and Eastern Galicia. After 1941, parts of the Soviet Union were also included.

German-Soviet Non-Aggression Pact: also known as the Molotov–Ribbentrop Pact, was named after the Soviet foreign minister Vyacheslav Molotov and the Nazi German foreign minister, Joachim von Ribbentrop. This pact guaranteed that the USSR and Germany would not attack each other, and temporarily awarded the eastern section of Poland to the Soviets. The Pact was important because it protected Germany from fighting on two fronts— until it was ready to continue its expansion to the east. Germany broke the pact with its attack (known as *Barbarossa*) on the USSR in June 1941.

Ghetto: the area of the city where Jews were forced to live was called a *ghetto.* These existed as far back as the early 1500s in Venice, Italy. Other major European cities created Jewish ghettos in the 1600s and 1700s. During the Third Reich, Jews were forced out of their homes into ghettos where the conditions ranged from inhumane to unsurvivable. The Germans established at least 1000 ghettos in German-occupied Poland and the Soviet Union.

Great Depression: caused in part by the U.S. 1929 Stock Market Crash, and lasting until the early 1940s, was a time of severe economic hardship. Businesses were forced to close, and hundreds of thousands lost their jobs, savings, homes, and farms.

Hashomer Ha-Tza'ir-Halutz: a Socialist, Zionist youth movement, founded in the 1920s in the Galicia region of the Austro-Hungarian Empire, that spread throughout Europe. Its members were trained for immigration to, and life in, Palestine, which had once been the Jewish homeland. With approximately 100,000 members, they were very active in anti-Nazi resistance.

Holocaust: also known as the *Shoah*, the Holocaust was the post-World War II name applied to Hitler's campaign to eliminate the Jewish People of Europe. "Holocaust Deniers" are people who say that the Holocaust never happened in spite of its indisputable authenticity.

Jewish Fighting Organization (ZOB): also known as the Jewish Combat Organization, was a World War II resistance group which, among other actions, was instrumental in engineering the Warsaw Ghetto Uprising.

Judenrat: a council of influential Jewish men, sometimes chosen by the Jewish community, but usually appointed by the Germans, who were forced to carry-out Nazi orders.

Mein Kampf: meaning "My Struggle," in German, is Adolf Hitler's two-volume autobiographical manifesto, written during his 1925–26 incarceration that followed his failed Beer Hall Putsch of November 1923. In it he outlines his beliefs that the Jews were a peril that must be eliminated.

Nazi: the abbreviation for the "National Socialist German Workers' Party" which, under Adolf Hitler, controlled Germany from 1933–1945. They called the years of their rule, "The Third Reich."

Nuremberg Laws: in 1935, at the annual Nazi meeting, the brutal anti-Jewish Nuremberg Laws were officially adopted by the German government. In defining who was a Jew, thereby differentiating Jews from Germans, these laws took German citizenship and human rights away from Jews. The post-World War II Nuremberg Trials, held between November 1945 and October 1946, were conducted by the Allies to prosecute and convict German war-criminals. The legacy of these trials is that national leaders would be held responsible for their countries' war crimes.

Ottoman Empire: founded in 1299, and by 1453 had become vast and powerful. It was dismantled in 1918 when it lost World War I to the Allies.

Modern-day countries that once were part of the Ottoman Empire include Turkey, Iraq, parts of Western Iran, Israel, Lebanon, Syria, Saudi Arabia, Kuwait, Bahrain, Qatar, Egypt, parts of Western Libya, and Sudan.

Pale of Settlement: was the far western territory of Russia—including former territories of Lithuania, Belarus, and Poland—where Jews were forced to live. The word "Pale" comes from the Latin *palus*, meaning "an enclosed area."

Partisan Combat Groups: clandestine, grass-roots groups of anti-German fighters who lived in the forests of Eastern Europe.

Passive Resistance: non-violent defiance of oppression.

Pogroms: (from the Russian word *gromit* for "violent destruction") were deadly, ongoing anti-Jewish riots that were first documented in 1821 in Odessa in what is now Ukraine. They became common in the Russian Empire starting in the late 1800s and continuing through the end of the Russian Empire at the end of World War I.

Polish Underground State: was comprised of two components. One was the government-in-exile, located first in Paris and then in London. The other component was the Underground Army on the ground in what had been Poland. While they worked closely together, many decisions had to be made independently by the group in Poland.

Propaganda: the deliberate creation and repetition of misinformation via various media in order to control and manipulate the perceptions, thoughts, and actions of others. The Germans' effective use of propaganda, as well as censorship, guaranteed that Germans would never read, hear, or see anything that was detrimental to the Nazi Party. This ensured that all but a very few German people would refrain from doubting or resisting the Nazis.

Resisters: for the purpose of this book, anyone who defied the Germans is referred to as a "Resister."

Righteous Gentiles: non-Jews who risked and often sacrificed their lives to help and to save Jews, are known as Righteous Gentiles, and honored at Israel's *Yad Vashem.*

Russian Empire: was one of the largest empires in history, existing from 1721 until after the Russian Revolution of 1917, when it was dissolved and replaced by the Union of Soviet Socialist Republics (USSR).

Shtetles: small Jewish villages that lived according to their own religious traditions. Author Sholem Aleichem's stories are set in a *shtetle*, as was the contemporary American musical, *Fiddler on the Roof*.

Stock Market Crash of 1929: during the 1920s the American Stock Market expanded far too rapidly, causing stock prices to peak and then suddenly fall, resulting in what was called a "crash." Spreading worldwide, businesses and banks closed, and millions of people lost all their invested money and savings, leaving thousands homeless.

Third Reich: Adolf Hitler's anti-Semitic Nazi German government from 1933 until 1945. Some consider the First Reich to have been the Holy Roman Empire from the 800s to the 1800s. The Second Reich refers to the German Empire which had existed from 1871 until 1918, when World War I ended.

Union of Soviet Socialist Republics (USSR): was a Communist-run country existing between 1922 and 1991. It was established following the defeat of the Russian monarchy in the Russian Revolution. It was governed from Moscow by Vladimir Lenin (1870–1924). After Lenin's death, Joseph Stalin soon came to power, and used brutality and terrorism to control the Soviet people from 1929, until his death in 1953. In 1991, the USSR was dissolved, and Russia once again became a country, with Boris Yeltsin as president.

Versailles Treaty: was signed between the defeated Germany and the victorious Allies in 1919, and required Germany to accept responsibility and punishment for the war. Since the Germans were not invited to the meeting where the Allies developed the Treaty's terms, the actual Treaty was dictated to them. This inevitably created the German nationalistic rage that Hitler exploited in order to start World War II.

Warsaw Ghetto Uprising: the valiant Jewish rebellion against the Germans which took place in Warsaw, Europe's largest ghetto. Over 400,000 Jews had been packed into less than two square miles of space. It began on April

19, 1943, and lasted until June 5, 1943, when the Germans burned the ghetto down.

World War I: began in 1914, when Archduke Ferdinand of the Austro-Hungarian Empire was assassinated by Serbians in Bosnia-Herzegovina at Sarajevo. Austro-Hungary retaliated against Serbia, and was joined by its partners Germany, the Ottoman Empire, and Bulgaria. They were known as the *Central Powers*. The Allies, also known as the *Triple Entente Powers* (French for friendship, understanding, and agreement), consisted of Great Britain, France, and eventually, Italy and the United States. The Allies defeated the Central Powers in 1918.

World War II: began on September 1, 1939, when Germany invaded Poland. Poland's allies, Great Britain and France, then declared war on Germany. The United States did not enter the war until after the U.S. Naval Base in Pearl Harbor, Honolulu, Hawaii was bombed by Japan on December 7, 1941.

Yad Vashem: the Holocaust Martyrs' and Heroes' Remembrance Authority was established by law in 1953, as Israel's official living memorial museum to both Jewish Holocaust victims, and Righteous Gentiles. As of 2013, there were 6,394 Polish Righteous Gentiles. At 25%, this is the highest number of Righteous Gentiles in all of Europe.

Yiddish: the Jewish/German language that originated around the 10th century in Eastern Europe. It includes some elements of Aramaic, Slavic, and Hebrew. In Yiddish it is called the *mame-loshn*, or "mother tongue."

Zionism: the international movement, founded in 1897 in Basel, Switzerland by Theodore Herzl, in order to create and maintain an official homeland for Jews in Palestine. This goal was achieved in 1948, with the defeat of the Arabs in Arab-Israeli War, and the establishment of the state of Israel.

From the Author

Joanne D. Gilbert

As a baby-boomer growing up in a predominantly Jewish suburb of Detroit, Michigan, my earliest childhood was influenced by my Grand-mother Millie's poignant stories of her beloved family and friends who had been murdered by the Germans in Vilna, Lithuania. In my childish inno-cence, I wondered why they didn't fight back. I also wondered why no one helped them. How did trains with humans packed in cattle cars go through towns and villages without anyone noticing? I was haunted by questions that no one I knew felt comfortable asking:

- Were the Gentiles really all Nazi collaborators?
- Did the Jews really "go like sheep to the slaughter"?
- Did European women—both Jewish and Gentile—defy the Nazis?

It wasn't until 2010, following a forty-year career in education, that I was finally able to begin exploring these questions. As part of this process, I traveled extensively, meeting and talking with Female Resisters and Partisans, who now are in their 90s. During these visits, I was impressed by how vital and beautiful they still are. As each began to speak, and the years evaporated, their buoyancy, strength, courage, wit, and determination never faltered. These interviews, which were more like conversations, would form the basis of my public-speaking presentations, and ultimately, this book.

While researching *Women of Valor: Polish Resisters to the Third Reich*, I have learned invaluable lessons about the human response to catastrophe. And I became particularly intrigued by the tendency of humans to try—at all costs—to hang on to their own humanity, by normalizing abnormal circumstances. When everyone around us shares the same challenges and hardships, it's hard to imagine that our circumstances actually might be unusual, or even horrific. For example, Americans who grew up during the Great Depression of the 1930s are often heard to say, "We were really poor, but we didn't know it because everyone else was just as poor. It was all we knew, so it seemed normal." Similarly, some children who are subjected to repeated abuse at the hands of adults or neighborhood bullies, might think their situation is normal, they may even blame themselves, thinking that they deserve their pain, and that there is no way out.

Furthermore, even if others try to tell us that our circumstances are dangerous or life-threatening, we might not believe them. We might think that at best, these messengers don't understand the situation, or at worst, they are meddling troublemakers, unworthy of our attention. Maybe we'd even like to silence these troublemakers for bringing unwelcome, outside information into our isolated world. We might feel paralyzed, and unable to try any alternatives. Too often, humans are terrified of the unknown, and instinctively strive to preserve that which feels familiar and therefore, normal.

Throughout history this amazing ability to adapt to our circumstances, has resulted in the survival of the species. How tragically ironic that this time-tested survival technique—trying to create normalcy from the abnormal—would become a death sentence for millions of innocent people in the 20th century. The very adaptability of the Jewish People, for example, which had served them well throughout centuries of oppression, is the same fiercely-determined adaptability that sealed their doom before and during World

War II. It prevented much of Europe's Jewish population (along with the rest of the world) from recognizing that Hitler's Final Solution to the Jewish Question was the historically unprecedented industrialization of death. The warnings and pleas of those who did recognize the impending Nazi Holocaust were too often unwelcomed and unheeded by those who steadfastly—and futilely—tried to normalize the abnormal by adapting to each degradation, each deprivation, and all too often, each death.

When I was growing up, it seemed normal that my family had no relatives other than my aunt, my Grandmother, and her two brothers. The rest of their immediate and extended family had perished in the Vilna Ghetto. It wasn't at all unusual that many of my friends had been born in the Displaced Persons' Camps throughout Europe. There was no need to question the number tattooed on the forearm of a beautiful and vivacious mom, who drove us to the movies on Saturday afternoons. None of us tried to engage the taciturn dad who limped because he had been shot in the leg while jumping from a concentration-camp-bound train. In many of my friends' darkened homes, a silent, suffocating pall guaranteed that certain questions would never be asked. And instead of space aliens and monsters, our childhood nightmares were populated by jackbooted Nazis. Throughout our safe, suburban American, baby boomer childhoods, along with Sugar Frosted Flakes, Howdy Doody, American Bandstand, and Hula-Hoops—there also roamed the ever-present phantoms of the Nazi Holocaust.

As teenagers, the legacy of the Nuremberg Trials compelled us to stand up against oppression. We rebelled against authority, joined the fights for women's rights, and civil rights, and protested the Vietnam War. So why was it that we never questioned the mythology of Jewish passivity during the Holocaust? Why didn't we question the mythology that European Gentiles were Nazis or collaborators? What a subconscious burden it was to grow up "knowing" that we were victims, and they were monsters. How powerfully these facts influenced our emotions, attitudes, decisions, relationships, and actions throughout our lives. How fortunate I have been to finally learn the truth, and how honored I am to be able to share it with others. The facts are clear and indisputable:

1. The Jews did not go "like sheep to the slaughter." They fought with every means available to save their lives and the lives of their loved ones and others.

2. The Polish Gentiles did not all collaborate with the Nazis. Thousands of them risked their lives and the lives of their loved ones to help the Jewish people of Poland.

3. Women of all ages played an important role in defying the Nazis.

Hopefully, the clarity that these answers finally bring to our historical, cultural, emotional and intellectual perspectives will inspire us to recognize oppression, and take effective action. It is not enough to proclaim, "Never Again!" We must strive to create a society where oppression cannot take root. Otherwise, future generations will look back on us and rightfully say that we were silent—that we stood by and did nothing.

Acknowledgments

From its inception, the Women of Valor Project has been blessed by happy coincidences that sometimes seemed more like miracles. The first occurred in spite of my erroneous life-long belief that the Polish people had been complicitous with Nazi Germany in its campaign to eradicate the Jews of Europe. I decided maybe it was time for me to challenge my beliefs by attending a traveling exhibit about Polish Resistance sponsored by the Galicia Jewish Museum of Krakow, Poland which was hosted by the University of Nevada/Las Vegas (UNLV). I was surprised when I learned that there actually were Poles who risked their lives to help Jews.

My misperception that Polish Jews had for the most part been passive during the Holocaust, and that Polish Gentiles had generally been bystanders or Nazi-collaborators, were not only inaccurate, but damaging. By keeping my perspective narrow, they had generated attitudes that prevented me from seeing reality, thereby affecting my emotions and behaviors in myriad ways. Once these beliefs were dispelled, I set out to learn as much as I could about the truth of Polish Gentiles and Jews. Particularly intrigued by the role played by the women in Poland, I began my quest to research, find, speak with, and document the stories of Jewish and Gentile women, who had not only defied the Nazis, but who had survived into their 80s, and 90s. Perhaps it was another miracle that so many of these women opened their homes and their hearts to me.

In the course of this project, I have also been honored and grateful to meet three highly accomplished, and extraordinarily kind, and humble men, each of whom could rightfully be described as a *mensch*, a Man of Valor. At the German Consulate in Los Angeles, I was warmly welcomed by the German General Consul, Bernd Fischer, who expressed appreciation for my work, and offered his assistance. Also in Los Angeles, at the American Jewish

University, I met with rabbi, author, and professor Michael Berenbaum, Ph,D., who patiently reviewed my manuscript, provided encouragement as well as essential corrections, and most graciously wrote the Foreword. In Ann Arbor, Michigan, forensic psychiatrist, author, and Holocaust Survivor, Dr. Emanuel Tanay, welcomed me warmly into his beautiful home, and helped me to understand the various facets and definitions of "resistance."

Along the way, many other wonderful people have helped me with this project by providing housing, financial and technical support, proof-reading, frequent heavy-lifting, invaluable contacts, moral-support and inspiration. These include my son, Greg, daughter-in-law, Christine, Granddaughter, Julia, my brother, Gary Ron, and my partner, jazz musician, Terry Ryan. Dear friends and colleagues who gave unselfishly of their time and support include: Linda and Emily Lulkin, Bess Levitt, Sharon and Arielle Gainsburg, Owen and Joan Kline, Sharon and Bart Rogow, Rick Dale, Janice Mantia, Susan Dubin, Esther Finder, UNLV History Professor and author, Michael Green, Ph.D.; Clinical Psychologist Charles Silow, Ph.D.; and the Honorary Polish Consul in Las Vegas, John Petkus. I am particularly grateful to my publisher, Steven Feuer, who founded Gihon River Press (www.gihonriverpress .com) in order to support Holocaust education by publishing Holocaust-related books. His belief in the merits of *Women of Valor: Polish Resisters to the Third Reich* has been unwavering. I am also indebted to Barbara Werden, for her encouragement, and graphic-layout skills.

I have sent many silent "thank yous" to three strong, and loving women, who sadly, are no longer with us. Each made such a profound impact on my childhood and teen years, that I feel they are still with me. I wish they could share my joy at having completed this book. They are my Grandmother, Micheleh (Millie) Wineman Ron, whose stories of the Vilna Ghetto were my first exposure to the Holocaust; Thelma Rosenbaum, my tenth-grade English teacher, who told me that I should become a writer; and Rosa Minc, whose life-long, love-story with her husband Max, which started when they were teenagers in the Warsaw Ghetto, showed me that love could transcend catastrophe.

As I embark upon my next book, *Women of Valor: French Resisters to the Third Reich*, I also thank my readers and audiences for their constant support and encouragement. I hope the *Women of Valor: Female Resisters to the Third Reich* series lives up to their ex-pectations, and encourages others to explore and celebrate Women of Valor.

Photo and Map Credits

Unless otherwise noted, all photographs are by the author, Joanne D. Gilbert. All maps are courtesy of the United Stated Holocaust Memorial Museum (USHMM) website: www.ushmm.org.

Front Cover: Individual photos courtesy of Lola Schwartz, Faye Schulman, Miriam Brysk, Manya Feldman
Back Cover photo of Joanne courtesy of Christine Zambrano Gilbert.

Page
27   Left photo courtesy of Mary Blowers, The Fleischman Residence, West
      Bloomfield, MI
      Right photo courtesy of Manya Feldman
41   Photo courtesy of Manya Feldman
57   Photo courtesy of Manya Feldman
61   Photo by Vivian Henoch, Editor, myJewishDetroit.org, courtesy of the
      Jewish Federation of Metropolitan Detroit
65   Photo courtesy of Faye Schulman
84   Photo courtesy of Faye Schulman
90   Photo courtesy of Faye Schulman
95   Photo courtesy of Faye Schulman
101   Photos courtesy of Lola Schwartz
111   Photo courtesy of Lola Schwartz
134   Photo courtesy of Lola Schwartz
135   Photos courtesy of Miriam Brysk
137   Photo courtesy of Miriam Brysk
158   Photo courtesy of Christine Zambrano Gilbert

Resources

Books

Brysk, Miriam, *Amidst the Shadows of Trees*, Gihon River Press: 2013

Gurewutsch, Brana, Editor, *Mothers, Sisters, Resisters: Oral Histories of Women Who Survived the Holocaust*, The University of Alabama Press: 1998

Laska, Vera, Editor, *Women in the Resistance and in the Holocaust: The Voices of Eyewitnesses,* Greenwood Press: 1983

Lieber, Lola, *A WORLD AFTER THIS: A MEMOIR OF LOSS AND RE-DEMPTION,* Devora Publishing Company: 2010

Lukas, Richard C., *The Forgotten Holocaust: The Poles under German Occupation 1939–1944*, Hippocrene Books: 2012

Ofer, Dalia and Weitzman, Lenore J., Editors, *Women in the Holocaust*, Yale University Press: 1998

Rappaport, Doreen, *Beyond Courage: The Untold Story of Jewish Resistance During the Holocaust,* Candlewick Press: 2012

Schulman, Faye, *A Partisan's Memoir: Woman of the Holocaust,* Second Story Press: 1995

Tec, Nechama, *Resistance: Jews and Christians Who Defied the Nazi Terror,* Oxford University Press: 2013

Organizations and Websites

Yad Vashem: www.yadvashem.org

United States Holocaust Memorial Museum: www.ushmm.org

Jewish Partisan Education Foundation: www.jewishpartisans.org

Jewish Women's Archive: www.jwa.org

www.jewishvirtuallibrary.org

www.polishresistance-ak.org

www.theholocaustexplained.org